A Week
on the
Lake

A Week
on the
Lake

ROGER LLOYD

A WEEK ON THE LAKE

iUniverse books may be ordered through booksellers or by contacting:

iUniverse
1663 Liberty Drive
Bloomington, IN 47403
www.iuniverse.com
1-800-Authors (1-800-288-4677)

ISBN: 978-1-4917-5493-1 (sc)
ISBN: 978-1-4917-5492-4 (e)

Printed in the United States of America.

iUniverse rev. date: 12/09/2014

IN MEMORIAM

Edward L Lloyd (1903-1959)
Martha Hall Lloyd (1906-1989)

Switzerland

Approaching my 75th birthday I felt an unexpected desire to go to Switzerland. Unexpected because I had not been to Switzerland for a long time nor had I for many years thought about the time I had spent there on the Lake of Geneva with my parents and my sister when I was a child. Now I felt a surprising urge to visit those scenes, the memories of which had been long submerged.

My parents loved Switzerland. They had friends there, now long since gone to their graves. We spent holidays on the lake at Vevey. In those years right after the Second World War Switzerland was a land of plenty in a Europe still wretched and grim. There were few tourists then, mainly Americans and not many of them. The Germans were struggling to revive a largely destroyed and impoverished country and the English were constrained by severe restrictions on the export of currency.

Even before our first summer there I remember my parents talking about Switzerland--Geneva, the lake, walking in the mountains, St Moritz in winter, summer picnics with the wine cooling in a patch of snow. Even the labels on their luggage seemed magical-- Baur au Lac, Beau Rivage, des Bergues. The latter name stuck in my mind even before I knew how to pronounce it. The picture on the label was of a mountain which could, with the slightest twist of the visual imagination, appear either as a dark peak framed by blue sky or as a jagged hole in the heavens, inducing a slight but sinister feeling of vertigo. The mountain was Mt Blanc and even at the debased level of a luggage label I must have sensed something of the mountain's mysterious power--the "still and solemn power" which Shelley perceived when he gazed at the mountain in 1816.

I suppose the first trip to Switzerland when my sister and I accompanied our parents must have been when I was eleven. Thereafter our trips to the continent became an annual occurrence until I went to college and began to have summer plans of my own. These family holidays almost always included a period by the great blue lake at the Grand Hotel at Vevey, My father having spent the war years in England, and post-War austerity almost matching that of wartime, sought the sort of luxury which only Switzerland could then supply, particularly good meals and fine wine served on snow-white tablecloths by attentive waiters. Our large American car would be caught up in a net and hoisted from the dockside at an English port to be lowered to the deck of the Channel steamer, and we would be off.

The journeys through France were always leisurely, and I remember very little of them. I do remember the terrain as flat and of little interest until we came to the slopes of Jura when the road climbed past terraced fields. I still marvel at the industry which built the stone retaining walls, so much more substantial than the cottages of those who built them. And then there was the descent to the lake, and Geneva.

After some time in Switzerland we might cross the Alps, and that I do remember clearly; climbing higher and higher to the pass over twisting roads which seemed very narrow. It was easy to imagine the hazards faced by early travelers, sometimes lost in snow storms--to be saved, we liked to think, by the monks of the Grand St Bernard and their huge dogs with little kegs of brandy hung around their necks. I remember the Grand St Bernard and one incident in particular which impressed me with the harshness of the high mountains and the austere life of the monks at that altitude. We had stopped the car at the monastery. I was standing alone--I imagine the rest of the family had gone to the shop where liqueurs, post cards and other tourist goods were sold. It was cold and even though it was high summer there were patches of snow on the ground. A monk approached me and indicated that I should follow him. He led me to a small house or hut of stone, windowless but with a low wooden door. He led me through the door. There on platforms were the bodies of deceased monks, still deep frozen. They seemed to me mere shrouded shapes; I could distinguish no features.

Descending to Italy we might go as far south as Naples. I remember wandering into the Galleria Umberto, then still in full possession of its wartime reputation as a haunt of criminals and prostitutes. Prim child as I was, and lacking the empathy that comes with experience, I was repelled by the crowd of importuning scarecrows—some crippled or deformed, noisy and leering and dressed in rags--that pressed around us. We must have been among the first real tourists after the War in that city, then so desperately poor and wretched.

*   *   *

It was not only the pursuit of childhood memories, though, which got me on the flight to Geneva. I had read about the summer of 1816 when the poets Byron and Shelley first met and of the time they spent together on the shores of the lake. In June they took a boat and made a circuit of the lake, a trip they recorded in letters and journals. Their voyage took them not only past the towns of Savoy, the mouth of the Rhone, Chillon, Vevey and Lausanne but also on an intellectual journey which would affect not only their friendship but their ideas and their art. I had the idea that I would follow them, not in a small boat but on the steamers which ply the lake, and attach their impressions and memories to my own.

And then there was the lake itself which, with all its associations, was a kind of cultural landmark. Lake Geneva (the Roman Lacus Lemanus, Lac Leman, Leman's Lake as the English tourists of the nineteenth century called it) was like a vast puddle in the middle of Europe through which flowed not only the waters of the Rhone but so much of the intellectual energies of the Enlightenment and the movement we call Romanticism. The shores of the lake were littered with reminders of the lives not only of Byron and Shelley but Rousseau, Gibbon and Mme de Stael. Byron himself felt this. In his sonnet dedicated to the "Lake of Beauty" he invokes Rousseau, Voltaire and Gibbon. While "sweetly gliding" on the crystal waters he felt the glow of the "not ungentle zeal", the proud legacy to him of these immortals which "makes the breath of glory real." There was enough here to stir the most languid and stay-at-home reader into becoming a cultural tourist.

These were the thoughts which drew me to Geneva at that time. So I came for a week at the end of August as the summer was dying.

Earlier States

Those summers in Switzerland were the summers of my late childhood, just before the years when I became the person I would remain. Now, on the flight to Geneva, peering through the airplane window at the glare from the snow-topped Alps, earlier memories came unbidden as in a dream. It was as if being put in mind of those summers in Switzerland led me to a deeper excavation of my past. Some memories came back to me with great clarity; others were elusive, like distant shapes in the sun's dazzle which found me squinting to make them out. They seemed to be an inescapable preface to my post-War memories of Switzerland and the quest that brought me back.

Searching for my earliest memories, which are fragmentary at best, I seem to recall my descent on a tricycle down a steep driveway, the sense of excitement mixed with a full apprehension of the inevitable fall. That was in Washington City before we came to England. But the earliest memories which are most distinct now all date from those months in England just before and after the declaration of war in Europe. Like a pageant in my mind I saw scenes played out drawn from those years and which taken all together make up the narrative of early childhood. In the earliest of these scenes a small boy is sitting on a window seat in London watching black barges moving up the Thames. The boy is me, five years old, the window seat is in a flat in Dolphin Square on the

Embankment and the barges are carrying coal to the Battersea Power Station. The picture is grey like an old photograph but the memory is real. The year is 1939.

That scene came vividly before my eyes again some seventy years after the original occurrence. I found myself in a London gallery looking at an 1896 lithograph by JAM Whistler of the Thames, the river he had so often depicted previously in paintings and prints. But this was different from his other views of the river. The scene was not uncommon, with barges on the water and dark industrial buildings on the opposite bank, all immersed in a grey mist. But to an uncanny degree the scene was exactly as it had been presented to my memory, though I had not seen this picture before. Not only the position of the boats and the impression of the water but the very tone and texture was as I remembered it. This may have had something to do with the fact that the Thames is shown at a point farther downriver from Whistler's usual position, from a place near the Strand rather than Chelsea or the Battersea Reach. There was also an unmistakable atmosphere of melancholy which suffuses both the picture and my early memory. In Whistler's case this would be due to his circumstances when he drew this scene. He had married in 1888 but eight years later his wife died of cancer. In her last days Whistler took rooms for them both in the Savoy Hotel and this picture, the last of his Nocturnes, was drawn from there. Whistler took great care in producing the stone and revising the image but after his wife's death he could not bear to have it printed. Impressions, such as the one I saw, were only made after his death.

Rumours of war were followed soon enough by war itself, and the year following my memory of Dolphin Square my father moved his office from London to Oxford where we lived in a rented house on Mansfield Road. From that time I remember my father upright, pole in hand, at the stern of a punt on the Cherwell, and teaching me to ride a bicycle.

Looking through the album of photos taken in 1940 it strikes me how gay, even jaunty, my parents—then in their early thirties—seem to be. Even the pictures showing signs warning of air raids, or of the children trying on their gas masks, do not dim the general impression. Only my sister and I wear solemn, even gloomy, expressions.

It surprises me to discover, thinking back to that time, how much my father featured in that chapter of my narrative; especially since, after the separation of the War years, he would re-enter my life as a different person--or, at least, seen from an altered perspective. Recalling him in a Cherwell punt brought back all the river images and smells--tea-colored water, drooping willows, flowered meadows at the water's edge--which for me represented a world and a life soon to be cut off. It was on one of my father's brief visits to his family during the War that he brought to the notice of his children that elegiac tribute to the river world, *The Wind in the Willows*. My father had a fine reading voice and as he read it one evening at my uncle's ranch I could not hold back the tears.

At that time there was one event I remember which in its strangeness might have prompted a sense of foreboding, of innocence threatened or, at the least, put on notice of realities lurking just out of sight. There was a place on the river where a portage was required, to avoid a weir. Our punt would be pulled over rollers across a spit of land to reenter the water on the other side. Not far from this place was a section of river bank set apart for (male) nude sun bathing, called Parson's Pleasure. While my mother and sister walked around the outside of this place my father and I took the path through it. There, and the memory comes back with such clarity, I was confronted by a man, probably some college don, gaunt to the point of seeming skeletal, wearing a trilby hat and nothing else. His skin had a yellowish tint and hung loose about his bones. Whatever his real state of health, he seemed to me an image of mortality, like the sick and aged man who confronted the young Gautama Buddha to call into question his artificial paradise.

It would be false to import, in retrospect, any consciousness on my part of a prophetic significance in this apparition, but I have one other memory of an event in Oxford in that year 1940 which is more concrete. I was awakened by the sound of voices and went from my bedroom to the landing at the top of the stairs. Looking down I saw a crowd of young men in miscellaneous types of clothing--parts of army uniform, sweaters of all colors. Later I learned that my father had found these men, who were soldiers returning after having been rescued from the beaches of Dunkirk, at the Oxford railway station. In a typically impulsive and generous gesture he had brought them back to our house for food and drink before they went on their way to rejoin their regiments, or what was left of them.

In the autumn of 1940, the War by then having reached a fiercer stage, my father was advised by the American Embassy to remove his family on what would be the last regular trans-Atlantic civilian sailing, on the SS Washington of the United States Lines. Taking this advice meant crossing to Ireland, since the Washington sailed from a neutral port at Galway. Passing through Dublin left me with one memory which for a long time I would have been happy to escape. While it might have been but another exposure to the fact of mortality, it became in my memory an experience in which the real and the imagined seemed to be confused, to the extent that I came to doubt that the experience actually occurred. I recalled a church in the crypt of which the bodies of the ancient dead were mummified. Some of them wore eighteenth or nineteenth century clothing. A cranky, gnome-like custodian was grinning as he invited me to shake the hand, now a leathery claw, of a two hundred year old corpse. I took the hand and looked in vain for evidence of former life in the withered, sunken face, eyeless, with jutting teeth from which the shriveled lips had withdrawn. This was a vision which haunted me for years. Only much later, in my middle age, did I discover that the church, St Michan's, actually existed. I was rummaging through some of my mother's papers and found a file containing souvenirs of that voyage in 1940--photos, a passenger list, menus and the like. There I was startled to find a post card of the church in Dublin which I at once recognized as the site of my ghastly experience. Later, finding myself in Dublin, I went looking for it. After some trouble I found it in a neighborhood of poor houses. The church appeared to be abandoned, in a scruffy yard full of weeds. The building was locked, but after knocking on several doors someone with a key was found. The way down to the crypt was through a narrow entrance. The dark chamber seemed, after the passage of forty years, to be tiny. The bodies of the dead were simply forlorn. But the old vision, the fuel of childhood nightmares, was put to rest.

My father soon went back to England where he remained, except for a couple of short visits, throughout the War. Without my father, we spent the war years at my uncle's ranch in Oklahoma. Those years seemed such a paradise to my sister and to me. Our Uncle Edmund, my mother's brother, always full of fun and laughter, was like a substitute parent, then having no children of his own. There was milk from the cow, eggs from the hens, clear water from the well, fruit and vegetables from the garden and, best of all, our own horses to ride--we even rode them to the local school. This all came to an end one day in town. Going to town was always a treat, since we did not make the journey over the rutted dirt roads more than once a week. The shopping done my sister and I would usually be given a quarter each for the movie and soda pop. But that fateful day there was no quarter, movie or pop. We were parked in a playground outside the house of our mother's friend, sitting disconsolately on a swing and wondering why we were still there. Suddenly the screen door slammed and mother came floating across the street, her cotton dress billowing behind her. "The War is over. We are going back to England."

Leaving the ranch after our happy years there was a sad affair, even for my mother who was so anxious to see her husband again. For us children it meant having to abandon our beloved animals, particularly our collie dog and my sister's Shetland pony, Queenie. While the dog remained at the ranch the pony was promised to another child. After we set off by car for the railway station, some miles down the road, we saw Queenie standing in a field looking at the road and seemingly bidding us farewell. She was in some ways a perverse and unruly creature but at that moment she seemed to share some of the regret at parting.

The return to England was by a roundabout route. We left Oklahoma by train, changing trains in Chicago. (For some reason it was impossible to go through Chicago without disembarking at one railway station, then taking a taxi to another station where trains left for points east.) Reaching New York there was another change of train for one bound to Quebec, where we boarded our ship for the Atlantic crossing, the RMS Britannic of the White Star Line.

Aboard the Britannic it seemed we were already in England such was its strangeness and austerity. The ship was full of returning evacuees, women and children. It had been converted to serve as a troopship during the War and retained that appearance. The doors had been removed from all the staterooms, replaced by flimsy curtains of florid chintz, presumably to aid rapid escape in the event of the vessel being torpedoed. There was a small gun mounted on the deck which, even to us children, seemed inadequate armament against any U-boat attack. Once at sea I scanned the grey Atlantic rollers looking for (hoping for?) the lean shape of a German submarine whose captain had refused to accept his country's surrender.

When the ship finally reached Liverpool my father met us at the dockside. He appeared a stranger to me then, unlike the person I remembered from what seemed such a gulf in time. Seen against the background of the Liverpool docks he struck me as foreign. This was fascinating to me and, in a way, delightful, emphasizing the strangeness of everything I saw that day.

My father quickly had us all organized, our luggage reclaimed from the ship's hold, and bundled us into taxis. We went to the Adelphi

Hotel, an Art Deco masterpiece in which a more discerning eye than mine might have remarked the shabbiness of the once grand public rooms. I only saw the grandeur, and if it seemed a bit faded that only added to the allure. The dining room, the elderly waiters, all impressed me. The crowning moment was my introduction to that uniquely English pudding, lightly dismissed as a "trifle", a sickly sweet mess of cake covered with (doubtless on that occasion synthetic) custard. It then seemed to me to be the most exquisite dish I had ever eaten, belying the warnings I had been given of the austerities of post-War Britain.

Arriving in Oxford we were installed temporarily in a residential hotel on Boars Hill just to the south of the city. My father had lived in digs throughout the War and had no fixed residence then. Before long a house was found, a red brick neo-Georgian house called Sunningwood, near the village of Sunningwell, with spacious views toward Abingdon and the distant Newbury Downs. This was to be our home for the next fifteen years.

My poor father, trying to resume family life which had been ruptured and with children who were wild and ill-educated strangers! He must have wondered how we were to be raised and broken in to English life. As for me, it was some time before I came to appreciate my father's nature in this his, as it were, second incarnation in my life. In place of the vague but affectionate image of him I had kept, he was now a fuller and more interesting presence. Our relations over the next few years were not always easy though. I know I exasperated him at times and there were moments when we seemed to have little to say to one another, times even when the affection we undoubtedly felt could not somehow fuse into adequate expression. Looking back now I can see that my father, while completely American, could also be seen as very Welsh; by which I mean that he was loquacious, inclined to be mercurial, sometimes pugnacious and emotional. He could be intolerant and, with me in those years, he had much to tolerate.

11

Since there was no school which would take me, at ten years of age and in my state of ignorance, a tutor was found for me. Of my time with the tutor I remember mainly that his ugly Victorian house in North Oxford was always bitterly cold and smelled of stale pipe smoke. There, at a table in his study, I struggled with Latin sentences and French irregular verbs, subjects of which my education, such as it was, had until that time been entirely innocent. All I remember of that time was discomfort and embarrassment, shame at my ignorance and, as my tutor doubtless saw it, my stupidity, and one humiliating occasion. Seated one day at his side at the table in his freezing room I saw a drop of moisture, the size of a quite valuable pearl, form and cling to the end of his somewhat narrow and pointed nose. I could not control my laughter and neither could I bring myself to answer truthfully his question--what was I laughing at? Now I can understand his anger. This must have been the final insult to a man who considered his task demeaning; the task, that is, of instilling the knowledge possessed by every normal English schoolboy into the thick head of a yankee yahoo. "Cheek! cheek!" he shouted as his resentment boiled over and he struck me, his fury bringing a glow of false warmth to his pallid jowls.

The mixed feelings of shame and amusement brought on by that memory were still with me when we landed. I shrugged them off on the way into Geneva.

III

Geneva, Shelley and Byron

Arriving in Geneva I settled myself in my small hotel near the lake, then walked along the lake front--past the statue of the Empress Elizabeth at the spot where she was so bizarrely murdered, past the quais where the steamers departed, down to the bridge over the Rhone where the river surges out of the lake at the foot of the upper town, on its way across France to the marshes and the sea. It was from this spot in 1840 that John Ruskin contemplated the Rhone which he saw rushing like a mountain stream in "bliss at recovering itself again out of the lake-sleep.." In the afternoon sunshine the river was, for me, despite the office buildings and the grand hotels on the water front, as vital as Ruskin saw it then.

On the island in the river sat the statue of Rousseau, the citizen of Geneva--a place he rejected, then reclaimed and which then rejected him and now reclaims him again. Passing Rousseau with a nod I crossed into the old town where the Mairie had been thrown open to the citizens. People gathered for sausages and wine in the ancient courtyard, a communal event of the kind Rousseau would have approved. I found a small restaurant nearby and had a Swiss meal, ordering cheese fondue, something I had not thought of eating for many years. It was rich and, I am sure, dreadfully unhealthy, quite disgusting and absolutely wonderful. The white

Swiss wine I had with it seemed appropriate too--light and innocent as Heidi.

*   *   *

The next morning, reminding myself of my mission of exploration, I took a bus from the center of town to the suburb of Cologny. From the village bus stop it is a short walk to the house which Lord Byron rented from Edward Diodati in 1816 shortly after he met Shelley. The Shelley party was in a more modest house rented from Jacob Chapuis just below the Villa Diodati, beside the lake at Montalegre. The site of the Chapuis house is now covered by suburban development. In 1816 vineyards clothed the hill and a narrow path through them led from the Maison Chapuis to the Villa Diodati. It could not have been more than a ten minute walk. Today the vineyards are gone, though there is a grassy field on the slope beside the Villa where the vines must once have been.

The Villa Diodati seems exactly as it was in 1816, a handsome house with cream-colored walls and broad balconies where Byron would sit and write at a small table. Nor has the view across the lake changed much. Beyond the rise of the hills on the other side of the lake the frayed edge of the distant mountains shows dark against the pale blue of the sky, all the way to the Cret de la Neige, highest peak in the Jura. This view of lake and mountains is just as it appeared to Byron. There have been changes on the periphery. Now the *jet d'eau* is visible leaping up from the Geneva harbor mole and the lake shore has more buildings than it did then. The lake is probably emptier of boats too, though on that sunny afternoon there were pleasure boats on the water. As I admired the view a two-masted schooner slowly crossed the lake, its sails almost limp in the late afternoon calm. One boat added a more contemporary note with its peach-colored sail making it resemble a large water spider. A solitary water skier was pulled across the lake. As the sun began to sink the light glittered on the lake surface like shards of glass on a table. The distant spire of Geneva Cathedral was a dark

outline against the heat haze. The city's murmur could only just
be heard. That was the only sound except for a jet taking off from
Geneva airport and, far off, the klaxon of a police car or ambulance
with its two repeated notes, rising and falling, insistently repetitive
like the song of an idiot child.

*　　*　　*

It now seems to us that Byron and Shelley were destined to meet
but in fact their lives had taken very different paths and but for
one amorous connection they might never have met at all. True,
they had much in common. They came from the same social class
and shared the usual education of that class (Harrow and Eton,
Cambridge and Oxford). They also shared radical political views.
But their lives and personalities were otherwise very different.
Though each, at times, expressed admiration for the poetry of
the other it was often with reservations. One great thing they
had in common was that each had left England under a cloud
of scandal and disgrace. For Byron his rejection by society was
painful. Shelley, on the other hand, thought of himself as rejecting
the norms of society for a higher ideal. But they both met under the
shadow of disapproval following wrecked marriages.

Shelley's radical views appeared early. As a schoolboy young Bysshe,
as he was then called, turned against his father, Sir Timothy Shelley,
a baronet and wealthy Sussex landowner, when he learned of the
corrupt, but at that time probably not so very unusual, methods by
which Sir Timothy had secured election as MP for East Shoreham.
This enmity persisted and was probably the psychological root of
Shelley's rejection of, and sometimes paranoid sense of persecution
by, all authority—priests, kings or even God. Shelley managed to
get himself sent down from Oxford, along with his friend Thomas
Jefferson Hogg, for publishing his views on religion in a pamphlet
provocatively entitled *The Necessity of Atheism*. Five months later he
eloped, aged nineteen, with the sixteen year old Harriet Westbrook,
the daughter of an owner of coffee houses and taverns in London.

Along with this rebellious behavior Shelley had well developed radical opinions, rejecting not only religion but the whole hierarchical and, as he saw it, repressive nature of society at the time, including the institution of marriage. For Shelley and those who shared his views William Godwin was a revered figure, both for his writings and for his defiance of the Pitt government's "gagging acts" in 1796. It was natural, then, that Shelley should write to Godwin seeking his encouragement and support. Godwin's reputation attracted a number of radicals to his house, including William Hazlitt and Leigh Hunt and even the American Aaron Burr who was Godwin's lodger in 1811.

Godwin's radical credentials had been enhanced by his marriage in 1797 to Mary Wollstonecraft. She had been a witness to the Revolution in France and had become a founder of modern feminism with the publication in 1792 of her *Vindication of the Rights of Woman*. She had loved, and been deserted by, the rascally American, Gilbert Imlay, by whom she had a daughter, Fanny. Clever and resourceful, Mary had, by the time she met Godwin, achieved some success as a writer in London. Godwin was shattered when she died of puerperal fever shortly after giving birth to their daughter, another Mary.

Deeply as he had loved Mary, this did not prevent Godwin from marrying again, which he did in 1801, just two years after Mary's death. As had been the case with Mary, the decision to marry was precipitated by the pregnancy of the bride. Godwin's second wife was Mary Jane Clairmont who had two children already; a boy, Charles, then five, and a girl of three, Jane, later always referred to as Claire. With the little boy William Godwin the Godwin household included five children.

Though Shelley wrote to Godwin in January 1812 as an admirer, eager to make the acquaintance of the veteran of English radicalism, Godwin saw Shelley in a very different light. Godwin by then was an impecunious bookseller with a large family to support. He had backed away from many of his earlier radical opinions. Godwin saw in Shelley not so much a disciple as a rich young man who might come to his aid financially and welcomed him for that reason. But Shelley had done very little to assist Godwin when, in the summer of 1814, he fell in love with Godwin's daughter Mary. By then Shelley was already estranged from his wife. Harriet was very pretty but not very bright. Shelley explained to his friend Hogg that there was more to life than "cultivating" Harriet. Once he fell out of love with her his feelings soon turned to disgust. He felt "as if a dead and living body had been linked together in loathsome and horrible communion."

Mary Godwin was a very pretty sixteen year old, but it may have been her radical antecedents that both attracted Shelley and seemed to sanction his adultery. Free love was the doctrine most commonly, and scandalously, associated with the Godwin/Wollstonecraft circle. It seems no accident that Shelley declared his love for Mary on one of the visits the pair made to her mother's grave in St Pancras churchyard. Mary's biographer, Miranda Seymour, even suggests that it was there that their love was first consummated: "The discrete north-eastern corner of St Pancras churchyard would have seemed an appropriate setting, as if Mary Wollstonecraft were presiding over their union. Her grave was conveniently shaded by willows."

Be that as it may, inevitable disturbances followed. Harriet, who was then pregnant with a second child by Shelley, was distraught. Shelley appealed to the radical principles endorsed by him in his *Queen Mab* (originally dedicated to Harriet, he sent a lovingly inscribed copy of the poem to Mary). Marriage should continue only so long as there was mutual love; "love is free." Mary's step-sister Claire acted as eager go-between. Mary, though deeply in love, was shocked by Shelley's insane behavior. He burst into her room with a bottle of laudanum and a pistol. She was to drink the laudanum and he said he would shoot himself. Godwin, whose views on marriage were no longer those of his youth, defended

17

Harriet as an "innocent and meritorious wife" and begged Shelley to spare the "fair and spotless fame of my young child," while at the same time importuning Shelley for a payment of 2,500 pounds which he believed he had been promised.

On 28 July, 1814, Mary and Shelley, with Claire in tow, took flight to Dover and, after a stormy crossing, arrived in Calais the following morning. The trio then proceeded, by carriage, on foot and by mule, across France to Switzerland. Shelley once more demonstrated his loose grip on reality by inviting his abandoned wife, by then five months pregnant, to join them, presumably to make up a happy kind of commune. When they reached Switzerland it became apparent they were running out of money and would have to return, which they did by way of the Rhine and Holland. After another stormy sea crossing they finally reached London. They did not have enough money to pay for their passage so, accompanied by a sailor deputed by the captain of the ship to keep an eye on them, they went around town trying to borrow the needed sum. At last Shelley went to his wife for a loan.

There followed a period of emotional disruption, financial penury and social ostracism. Shelley refused to return to his wife and lost all further support from that quarter. Mary was disowned by her father, which she saw as a denial of her mother's principles. Godwin condemned Shelley as the seducer of his daughter, but accepted money from him whenever Shelley could get it. Shelley's friends refused to see him, except for Thomas Love Peacock and the faithful Hogg. Claire refused to go home and became increasingly hysterical and erratic. It is most likely that Claire was in love with Shelley and jealous of Mary (she was amazed that they seemed to spend so much time in bed). Mary also flirted with Hogg, encouraged by Shelley. This stormy period came to an end when Mary's child was born and soon after died. The notion of some kind of free love commune was abandoned. Claire was exiled to a cottage in Devon, much to Mary's relief.

In January 1816 Mary gave birth to her second child, William. Claire returned to London to help her. It also gave Claire the chance she had been looking for to seduce Lord Byron.

*   *   *

Byron at that time was at a low ebb. He was living in his set of rooms in Albany, having left his house at 13 Piccadilly Terrace when his marriage collapsed. On January 15th Lady Byron had left London with their child, Ada, to visit her parents. She wrote a cheerful and loving letter to him, couched in the playful private language they sometimes used. Later she said it was written merely to deceive him as to the way things stood while she had doctors assess his sanity. Then on February 2nd she wrote to him demanding a separation. Byron staggered from the shock. Soon rumors, true and false, began to swirl around him, accusations of adultery, sodomy, incest--and insolvency (there were bailiffs in the house). The *beau monde* turned against him. Byron, when Claire first approached him, was not in the mood for flirtation. But, as he had confessed to his friend and confidante Lady Melbourne in 1812, "I could love anything on earth that appeared to wish it."

Claire's letters to Byron are very amusing now, the naive deceptions of an eighteen-year-old would-be *femme fatale*. She cast fly after fly trying to get the sluggish fish to rise. She tried the role of an unnamed noble lady smitten with love for the author of *Childe Harold*, stamping her letter with a seal Shelley had given her to add credence to the aristocratic pretense. Then she wrote as an aspiring actress, later as a playwright seeking his help, since he was a member of the Committee of the Drury Lane Theatre. Finally Claire managed to achieve a meeting. Byron wrote, in March or April (to "GCB", one of Claire's aliases): "Lord Byron is not aware of any 'importance' which can be attached by any person to an interview with him--and more particularly by one with whom it does not appear that he has the honour of being acquainted--He will however be at home at the hour mentioned." Claire threw herself at him and achieved the desired result. She proposed an assignation somewhere in the country, a suggestion Byron rejected. He was on the point of leaving England and had no time for such intrigues. They did have sexual intercourse, at last, on April 20th. In her old age Claire claimed it was in a house in Albemarle Street and Lady Byron had seen them enter it. On April 21st Byron signed the Deed of Separation. On the 23rd he left London for Dover, accompanied by his friends John Cam Hobhouse and Scrope Davies, who went to see him off. Contrary winds delayed his departure and he finally sailed into exile on the morning of the 25th,

Claire had used the Shelley connection to arouse Byron's interest in her. Byron was an admirer of Godwin and had praised *Queen Mab*. Claire managed to achieve a meeting between Byron and Mary. They took to one another. Perhaps Byron, who was being shown the cold shoulder by the fashionable hostesses who had previously courted him, felt a kinship with another who had been punished for offending respectable society. Claire sensed that her connection with Shelley was the way to stay close to Byron. Claire had written to Byron, "On Monday you go for Italy and I--God knows where." Byron had no wish to take Claire with him, but Claire knew Byron was going to Italy by way of Switzerland and hatched a plan to join him in Geneva. Byron had written to Lady Holland in March, "It is my intention to proceed by way of Geneva--but to make no great delay in Switzerland--as my wish is to get to Rome and see as much of the rest of Italy as I can." Shelley and Mary were also going to Italy. Claire persuaded them to go by way of Geneva. Shelley, Mary, Claire, with little William and a nurse, Elise, crossed the Channel a week after Byron.

Claire had one other means to attach herself to Byron, though he did not yet know it. When she left England she was pregnant.

*   *   *

Byron travelled with his usual servant, Fletcher, and the physician, Dr John W Polidori, who had been offered 500 pounds by Byron's publisher, John Murray, to write an account of their travels. In Byron's huge Napoleonic traveling coach, which broke down frequently, the party trundled across Europe towards Switzerland via Ghent, Bruges, Brussels, the field of Waterloo (where Byron picked up souvenirs of the battle and over which he galloped on a Cossack horse left behind by "some of the Don gentlemen") and the course of the Rhine. As Byron progressed, nursing feelings of hurt, bitter resentment and rejection, he might also have felt some relief, a sense of escape. *Childe Harold*, the poem he brought back from his Eastern travels in 1811, and which made him an instant celebrity on its publication, was all about the escape of travel, Harold getting away from the mess and frustration of his life in England to find himself as a wanderer in the world.

The extraordinary success of *Childe Harold* was not, of course, due simply to its evocation of the delights of travel to exotic places. If the form (a travel book in verse) was original, so was the language. Tom Moore wrote that Byron was "as much the child and representative of the Revolution, in poesy, as another great man of the age, Napoleon, was in statesmanship and warfare." But it was the character of the Childe narrator, easily conflated with the personality of the poet himself, that caught the attention of everyone, those traits of personality to which we give the name Byronic. A reviewer noted that there was "something piquant in the very novelty and singularity of that cast of misanthropy and universal scorn, which we have...noticed as among the repulsive features of the composition." It was the singularity rather than the repulsiveness which made the deepest impression. Byron's personal appearance contributed to the cult. *Childe Harold,* as Elizabeth, Duchess of Devonshire wrote in 1812, "is on every table, and himself courted, visited, flattered, and praised wherever he appears. He has a pale, sickly, but handsome countenance, a bad figure, animated and amusing conversation, and, in short, he is really the only topic almost of every conversation--the men jealous of him, the women of each other." Byron's pallor may have been caused by his severe dieting regime--soda water and purgatives--and his "bad figure" might be a reference to his lameness, but as the Duchess suggests these features only made him more fascinating.

Byron received huge numbers of letters from adoring female fans. Since he kept the letters--and the locks of hair often enclosed, making up a large bundle--one can only assume that Byron was flattered by all this attention, particularly since some of the letters revealed a remarkable degree of sexual excitement. Byron enjoyed a number of fleeting seductions of some of these women, but two affairs affected his future profoundly.

Byron called Lady Caroline Lamb his "evil genius." She was three years older than Byron. Born Caroline Ponsonby she was the daughter of the Countess of Bessborough whose sister, the beautiful Georgiana, had married the Fifth Duke of Devonshire. Since the Countess had been paralyzed by a stroke early in Caroline's childhood, Caroline was brought up with her cousins in Devonshire House, Piccadilly, in the random fashion not uncommon in the aristocracy, a combination of luxury and neglect. In this world girls were thought not worth educating or bringing up, really, at all in any purposeful way. In spite of, or because of, such neglect, the result was often imagination and creativity, as well as a kind of wayward originality. As Caroline described her childhood it was one of "children neglected by their mothers...no one to attend to them--servants all at variance--ignorance of children on all subjects--thought all people were dukes or beggars--or had never to part with their money--did not know how bread, or butter, was made--wondered if horses fed on beef--so neglected in her education, she could not write at ten years old." And yet, Caroline filled her commonplace books with drawings and poems. Thin, nervous, imaginative, highly-strung, rebellious--her nicknames capture the wildness of her character: Sprite, Young Savage, Ariel, Little Fairy Queen.

In 1820, at the age of twenty, Caroline married the rising politician, William Lamb, son of Lord Melbourne. He would eventually become

Queen Victoria's favorite Prime Minister. But Caroline's domestic life was not altogether happy. Her first child was stillborn and her second, Augustus, was epileptic. She was ready to seek consolation outside her marriage. Caroline met Byron in his first flush of fame, at Holland House in Kensington where Byron was a frequent guest, and by the summer of 1812 they were lovers.

Caroline's hectic nature, her nervous recklessness, added to her obsession with Byron, combined to bring her to the border of hysteria. Her erotic life was already complicated enough. William Lamb was a flagellator. He had acquired a taste for *le vice Anglais* at Eton where he enjoyed being whipped and wished his tutor had flogged him more. He "amused himself," according to Caroline, "with instructing me in things I need never have heard or known." The disgust she first felt in a short time "gave way to a general laxity of principles which little by little...has been undermining the few virtues I ever possessed." Whatever were the things in which her husband instructed her, Caroline was certainly addicted to cross-dressing, frequently putting on the scarlet and brown livery she designed for her pages. This boy masquerade may have been calculated to appeal to Byron, with his homosexual tendencies, but he was at first lukewarm in his response to Caroline's advances. According to Caroline's friend Lady Elizabeth Auckland Byron "had no passion--used to keep Lady Caroline off, she by her own expression, being always making an offer of herself to him." Byron would make excuses: "no-no-not this evening" and the like, and remind her of her wifely obligations. When the consummation finally came it was surrounded by the macabre apparatus which was allegedly necessary to excite Byron's desire. It was "almost incredibly absurd--her head resting upon a skull, a case of loaded pistols between them." This sounds more like something Caroline would have contrived than anything thought up by Byron. (But, then, Byron was not averse to the occasional Gothick gesture; as a youth he liked to drink from a cup made from a monk's skull.) Whether or not any such flummery was necessary to excite Byron, Caroline was driven by a masochistic slavishness. She assured Byron

later that "I lov'd you as no woman ever could love because I am
not like them but more like a beast who sees no crime in loving and
following its Master--you became such to me--Master of my soul."

In the end Caroline's obsessiveness, the intricate masquerade of
female and male, page and master, slave and possessor, became
wearisome; and a bit frightening too. Byron was unable to get rid of
her. She threatened his position and his solitude. She broke into his
chambers in male dress. She pilfered the office of his publisher. She
threatened suicide or murder. She became increasingly deranged.
She sent him a packet of her pubic hair, stained with her blood.
As her behavior grew ever more strange she became, according
to her cousin, "worn to the bone, as pale as death and her eyes
staring out of her head." She was packed off to the Bessborough
estate in Ireland from whence she continued to bombard Byron
with passionate letters. She continued to write to Byron when she
returned to England even though he was by then finding relief in
the arms of Lady Oxford. Byron wrote to Caroline "I am no longer
your lover; and since you oblige me to confess it, by this truly
unfeminine persecution--learn, that I am attached to another...I
offer you this advice, correct your vanity, which is ridiculous; exert
your absurd caprices upon others; and leave me in peace." It is hard
to imagine a more comprehensive dismissal, even though, in view
of the sexual ambivalence at the heart of their affair, the accusation
of lack of femininity is a bit rich. Caroline's response was typically
stagey. She ordered a bonfire to be lit and arranged for a chorus of
village girls dressed in white to dance around it. One of her pages
recited her verses condemning Byron while she cast into the flames
a replica of Byron's miniature, copies of his letters, chains, rings,
flowers, feathers and other mementoes of her passion.

In the early summer of 1813 Lady Oxford left for the continent with
her husband, leaving behind a huge amount of gambling and other
debt. She had been forty to Byron's twenty-four and, after Caroline,
he had found her "autumnal charms" soothing. She was renowned
for her intelligence, her wit, her beauty, her radical politics and

her promiscuity. Her children, in view of their various paternity, were referred to as the Harleian Miscellany, the name given to the famous collection of early manuscripts assembled by Robert Harley, the First Earl of Oxford. After her departure Byron amused himself briefly by playing at seducing Lady Frances, the young wife of his friend Wedderburn Webster, but mainly for the pleasure of writing about it to Lady Melbourne, in a manner somewhat reminiscent of Choderlos de Laclos. But by July Byron was involved in the second of the great affairs which would affect the direction of his life, that with his half-sister Augusta Leigh.

*   *   *

Augusta and Byron shared the same father, "Mad Jack" Byron, and had known one another as children. Byron wrote affectionate letters to her from Harrow. By 1813 Augusta was married to her cousin, George Leigh, a colonel in the Hussars. He was a racing man, a gambler, and was more often at some race course than he was at home, though he had been attentive enough to his wife to give Augusta several children. Col Leigh had been an equerry to the Prince of Wales who had given to the Leighs The Lodge at Six Mile Bottom a few miles from Newmarket. Later, Leigh and the Prince had quarreled when Leigh had held on to some of the money he received for a horse he sold for the Prince.

In July and August of 1813 Byron spent time at Six Mile Bottom and undoubtedly he and Augusta slept together. Byron was in love. It is harder to know what Augusta felt exactly. She was naive to the point of foolishness, almost empty-headed at times. Byron's nickname for her, "Goose," seems particularly appropriate. For Byron the affair had the attraction of illicitness. It fell in with the Romantic culture of defiance and rejection of social norms. Byron added Augusta's hair to his, by now extensive, collection, labeling it "La Chevelure of the *one* whom I most *loved*." He marked it with a cross, their love symbol. Byron wrote of his love for Augusta that it had "a mixture of the *terrible* which renders all other--even passion (pour les autres) insipid to a degree." There was also the fact that he felt comfortable with Augusta. He relaxed with Augusta. Later, when he had gone into his continental exile, he confided to her that he had a daydream of them living chastely together like the Ladies of Llangollen. She seemed companionable and unchallenging, particularly after Caroline Lamb. Caroline was still making mischief in July. Seeing Byron at a party in London she brandished a dinner knife and threatened to kill herself.

I have often thought of Byron and Augusta when driving through Six Mile Bottom. For that matter even George Leigh, and the Regency plungers of his stripe, have appeared to my imagination on Newmarket Heath. The village of Six Mile Bottom is almost nothing; three or four cottages, a railway crossing and a pub, the same hostelry where Charles II and the Earl of Rochester paused on their all-night coach journeys from St James's to Newmarket. The Lodge is about a quarter of a mile north of the village, a substantial if somewhat bleak house of white-painted stucco surrounded by railed paddocks. I have been to the house only once and that was accidental, but an occasion not easily forgotten. It was a Sunday morning in winter. I was driving from Newmarket. It was cold but clear, a typical East Anglian morning. The reflection of the low sun glared off the road. A car darted out from a hidden drive and I applied the brake. My car spun on the ice, in slow waltz time, and left the road. The whole thing must have taken no more than an instant but it seemed slow, so slow, as the car plunged through the roadside hedge and buried its nose in the grass at the edge of a field. With thick trees growing in the hedge on either side of the point of entry, had the car gone through a few feet to right or left I would probably not be writing this. I left the car and walked to the Lodge, which is now an hotel. A low murmur of conversation came from the direction of the bar where guests were preparing themselves for lunch. I told the manager what had happened and offered to pay for the damage to the hedge. He nodded a wordless acquiescence, as if this were a daily occurrence, and let me use the telephone. As I waited for the breakdown lorry I looked around the house. Apart from two bad reproduction portraits of Byron and Augusta there was nothing to suggest their former presence. The impression was one of cold drafts and sparse occupation, almost desolation. It was hard to imagine it as being very welcoming, even as a family house in the summer of 1813.

In January, 1814, Byron and Augusta were at Byron's decrepit, Gothic family house, Newstead Abbey, near Nottingham. On April 15th Augusta gave birth to a daughter, Medora, widely assumed to be Byron's. In July they were holidaying together at Hastings. By the autumn Byron felt he was approaching some kind of crisis. He was still trying to shake off Caroline Lamb and his affair with Augusta could go nowhere. His two doomed and scandalous relationships had brought him to a state of near despair. The only way out seemed to be a respectable marriage, though he approached it with little enthusiasm. (The year before he had written: "I never see one much improved by matrimony. All my coupled contemporaries are bald and discontented.")

The chosen candidate was Ann Isabella (known as Annabella) Milbanke. The choice was approved by Byron's confidante and friend, Lady Melbourne. Annabella's father, Sir Ralph Milbanke, was Lady Melbourne's brother. Annabella at first refused Byron, but by the Autumn of 1814 she was free to accept him. Augusta was urging Byron to marry as a way out of his emotional torments and, in September when Byron was again at Newstead with Augusta, he wrote to Annabella. By the 18th of that month he was engaged.

Annabella was decorous, religious, intelligent and somewhat prudish. She was well educated and wrote poetry which was certainly literate if not inspired. As recognition of her learning Byron referred to her as the "Princess of the Parallelograms." She was pretty, if short and a bit on the dumpy side. When Byron met her for the first time in 1812 he described her, in a letter to Caroline Lamb, as "too good for a fallen spirit to know or wish to know, and I would like her better if she were less perfect."

Annabella's expectations from Byron can be sensed from the list of requirements for her ideal husband which she prepared at the invitation of Lady Melbourne. Along with principles of duty, generous feelings, freedom from habitual ill-humor, the manners of a gentleman and satisfactory levels of wealth and social status, she listed "an equal tenor of affection," but not "violent attachment." Byron was baffled when shown this list, as well he might be, but at least there was no danger of violent attachment. "As to *Love*," he wrote, "that is done in a week (provided the lady has a reasonable share) besides, marriage goes on better with esteem and confidence than romance, and she is quite pretty enough to be loved by her husband, without being so glaringly beautiful as to attract too many rivals." With these modest requirements of affection Byron and Annabella might have got on quite well. The problem was that Byron was only marrying because he felt he needed to and Annabella was marrying Byron because she saw the opportunity of reforming the famous poet. She saw it as her mission to redeem him from a life of dissipation. As Byron later said, "She married me from vanity, and the hope of reforming and fixing me."

Annabella's intentions were well meant. In a poem of 1814 she wrote

> Let my affection be the bond of peace
> Which bids thy warfare with remembrance cease,
> Blest solely in the blessings I impart,
> I only ask to heal thy wounded heart...

And Byron was not, at first, unreceptive. On the day Annabella accepted him he wrote to Lady Melbourne: "I mean to reform most thoroughly & become 'a good man and true' in all the senses of these respective & respectable appellations--seriously--I will endeavour to make your niece happy..." and a week later he wrote to Annabella asking her to "forgive my weaknesses--love what you can of me & mine--and I will be--I am whatever you please to make me."

This repentant and submissive mood was not to last. Doubts soon intruded. After Annabella accepted him Byron did not exactly rush to join her at her family home at Seaham in County Durham. After carving his and Augusta's names into the bark of an elm tree in the Devil's Wood at Newstead, Byron left for London. There he dawdled for a while. Then he went to Six Mile Bottom to be with Augusta before finally turning up at Seaham. It was perhaps Annabella's quiet scrutinizing of his character which led Byron at this time to write to Lady Melbourne: "I like them [women] to talk, because then they *think* less. Much cogitation will not be in my favour...I am studying her, but can't boast of my progress in getting at her disposition..However the die is cast; neither party can recede; the lawyers are here--mine and all--and I presume, the parchment once scribbled, I shall become Lord Annabella." Nothing could make clearer than this sardonic remark Byron's resentment at being remodeled and the threatened suffocating closeness.

After Byron tried to bed his intended, which was successfully resisted, Annabella suggested Byron return to London. Instead, he went to Six Mile Bottom. He wanted to break off the engagement but Augusta dissuaded him. The wedding, when it came, was anything but joyous. Hobhouse, Byron's best man, traveling with Byron to Seaham, thought Byron showed "indifference, almost aversion" at the prospect. On their honeymoon, or "treacle moon" as Byron called it, Byron woke in the middle of the night and, seeing the red glow of the candle light through the bed curtains, shouted "Good God! I am surely in hell!"

In retrospect it is easy to see the marriage as doomed from the start, but there were times when he couple were genuinely happy. Byron was delighted when his daughter Ada was born. They moved into the rented house in Piccadilly Terrace. Soon, however, the strains began to show. Byron spent more time at the Drury Lane Theatre, or with his friends, away from Annabella. He was frequently drunk and fell into rages. There were money troubles. Most of all, Byron could not resist teasing Annabella by emphasizing his wickedness, his sexual conquests, his incest and sodomy.

It would be wrong, I think, to believe that Byron's bisexuality was at the core of the failure of his marriage, though he used hints of it as a way of tormenting Annabella. At Cambridge Byron had fallen in love with a young chorister, John Edleston, one of the great lost loves of his life (but chaste, he assures us) with whom he had exchanged love tokens and to whom, as "Thyrza", he had dedicated some of his most moving verses. Edleston had died in 1811. Six of Byron's elegies to Thyrza were published as additions to *Childe Harold* in 1812, four of them written before Edleston's death. They were widely admired. Mary Godwin inscribed several verses of the poem *To Thyrza* in the precious copy of *Queen Mab* which Shelley had given her. Thyrza was assumed to be a woman and many of Byron's female readers associated themselves with Thyrza. Any doubts that Edleston was Thyrza were dispelled in 1974 when a seventh elegy was discovered, addressed to "te, te, caro puer" and superscribed, in Byron's hand, "Edleston, Edleston, Edleston." But at the time some women could imagine themselves to be the mysterious Thyrza, even though Thyrza was clearly dead. Lady Falkland wrote to Byron in 1812 assuming that she was intended as Thyrza. She would not have been rash enough to suppose herself Thyrza, she wrote, did not the date of Thyrza's death "exactly correspond with a severe illness, under which I was, at that time suffering--and indeed was almost reduced to the state you there so pathetically describe." Annabella herself, in an unpublished poem, "Thyrza to Lord Byron," written at the time of their courtship, identified herself with Thyrza, but a Thyrza brought back to life with the mission of reforming Byron and setting him on the path to redemption. This ghost of Thyrza firmly instructs Byron not to indulge in "...the selfish dream / That broods o'er unforgotten joy." These passions of the heart are merely the "dross of poor humanity." Instead, Byron should find in religion the "talisman of Happiness":

> No sympathy my shade can feel
> In thoughts to human passion given
> But would'st thou to my presence steal
> Direct thy chastened strain to Heaven.

One wonders what Annabella would have thought had she known that Thyrza was a boy. One wonders equally what Byron thought of Edleston transformed into Annabella out to reform him. It is easy to imagine the inward mirth Byron got from telling Annabella "I think I love you--better even than Thyrza," and showing her his collection of hair cut from his various lovers, including Edleston's.

Byron's homosexual, or, more precisely, paederastic, experiences went beyond his love for Edleston and crushes at Harrow. At Cambridge Byron was close to Charles Skinner Matthews and his circle of "Methodists" (ie, homosexuals) and easily fell in with their attitudes--jokey, clever and scandalous--of a kind familiar in universities then and now. Members of these circles were not necessarily resolutely "gay" as we understand it now and in no way precluded heterosexual steadiness in later life. Schools and universities were all-male establishments then and the Greek and Roman classics being so central in education references to love affairs with boys were part of the curriculum. Chasing after boys, with a bit of recreational buggery, carried the thrill of being outrageous and could be discreetly boasted about when indulged in abroad without risk of the penalties of the law, like smoking hashish in Nepal in the hippy era of the 1960's. Byron, in his letters from Greece referred to sex with his locally-recruited catamite and, with a nudge and a wink, to Horace. In June 1811 Byron wrote to his friend Hobhouse asking him to tell Matthews that "I have bade adieu to every species of affection and may say with Horace 'nec jam nec femina' etc, he will finish the lines." I conjecture that Byron was misquoting Horace's ode (the first of Book IV) which reads "Me nec femina nec puer iam nec spes animi," etc in which the poet begs Venus to release him from the pangs of love for girl or boy, though he dreams at night of embracing Lygurinus. The stanzas expressing passion for Lygurinus were considered risky enough to be indicated by discrete asterisks in Lord Lytton's high Victorian translation of the Odes.

In 1811, when Byron returned from the East, this youthful indulgence in paederasty came to an end, perhaps brought about by factors apart from the flood of excited female attention. There was a police raid on a homosexual haunt and a number of men were charged with "assault with the intention to commit sodomy" and sentenced to be pilloried in the Haymarket. The public was seized with a kind of homophobic terror, one among many such outbreaks of vengeful Puritanism which erupted from time to time in English life right own to the latter part of the twentieth century. It is only fairly recently that it is thought unacceptable that men should be criminally prosecuted on grounds of erotic preference and punished for a matter of temperament. Byron's friend Matthews was mysteriously drowned while bathing alone in the Cam. One suspects suicide. It was explained that he became entangled in weeds on the river bottom, which sounds implausible. Byron wrote despairingly to Scrope Davies that "Some curse hangs over me and mine... one of my best friends is drowned in a ditch." (Byron's mother had died at about the same time.)

Byron also enjoyed tormenting Annabella with cruel and mocking references to his other wicked inclination, his love for his sister. He alluded to his previous sexual relations with Augusta. When they visited Augusta at Six Mile Bottom Byron lay on the sofa and instructed Annabella and Augusta to take it in turns kissing him, Augusta's kisses being reciprocated more warmly than Annabella's.

By 1816, when the marriage was at the point of breakdown. the accusations swirling around Byron's head included cruelty, drunkenness, infidelity, sodomy and incest. In a curious alliance Caroline Lamb offered to share her scandalous stories with Annabella, anecdotes of Byron's boasting of his "ease of conquest" of Augusta and homosexual adventures on his travels. According to Hobhouse the accusations "struck at the very existence of Lord Byron as a member of society." Byron complained to Annabella that "my name has been completely blasted as if it were branded on my forehead." Already treated as an outcast, Byron signed the Deed of Separation and left for Dover.

It is easy to outline a speculative interpretation of the marriage drama. Byron understood at once what a mistake his marriage was and sought escape by driving Annabella out of it. The suppression of this, possibly unconscious, motive would leave him free to assume the mien of hurt and outrage--genuine in that he found himself cut off from the world in which he had been such a glamorous player. And yet, there was real regret on both sides. Perhaps the most revealing, almost wistful, prophetic epitaph of the Byron marriage are the *bouts-rimés* lines written by Byron and Annabella at Seaham in the early months of 1815:

> B: My wife's a vixen spoilt by her Mama
> A: Oh how I pity poor hen-pecked Papa
>   The Lord defend us from a Honey Moon
> B: Our cares commence our comforts end so soon.
>   This morn's a first time of many a happy year--
> A: I could not live so long with you, my dear
> B: O ever in my heart the last and first--
> A: And without doubt--it is the very worst.
> B: If rhymes be omens what a fate is ours--
> A: And bread and butter eagerly devours.
>   My husband is the greatest goose alive
> B: I feel that I have been a fool to wive.
> A: This weather makes our noses blue
> B: Bell--that but rhymes an epithet for you.

The couple mock each other. Annabella later recalled "making *bouts-rimés* together in the drawing room with that sort of mirth which seeks to jest away bitter truths." To Byron's sentimental, if not insincere, protestations of affection and regret at the dashed hopes for the "comforts" of marriage, though at the same time admitting he had been "a fool to wive," Annabella responds with disillusioned resignation. The "bread and butter" of domesticity was not for them.

The Summer of 1816

On May 13, 1816, Shelley, Mary, Claire and baby William arrived at the Hotel Angleterre beside the Lake at Secheron, just outside Geneva. On the 25th Byron arrived with Dr Polidori. They got in late at night and Byron, required to enter his age in the hotel register, wrote "100" and collapsed into bed, a bed Claire was soon invading. As Byron confessed in an apologetic letter to Augusta, it was hard to "play the Stoic with a woman who had scrambled eight hundred miles to unphilosophize me." Polidori recorded the first meeting with Shelley in his diary: "Getting out [of a boat] LB met M Wollstonecraft Godwin, her sister, and Percy Shelley...Dined: PS, the author of Queen Mab came: bashful, shy, consumptive, twenty-six: separated from his wife: keeps the two daughters of Godwin who practise his theories; one LB's." Shelley did not, in fact, have tuberculosis though his wild eyes and somewhat vivid complexion gave that impression. By June 3rd the Shelley party had moved into the Chapuis house and on June 10th Byron and Polidori took up residence at the Villa Diodati. The two households soon adopted the way of life they would pursue for the rest of the summer. Mary later provided a description of it to Tom Moore, who put it in his biography of Byron:

> At Diodati his [Byron's] life was passed in the same regular round of habits into which, when left to himself, he always naturally fell: a late breakfast, then a visit to

the Shelleys' cottage and an excursion on the Lake;--at five dinner (when he usually preferred being alone), and then, if the weather permitted, an excursion again. He and Shelley had joined in purchasing a boat...a small sailing vessel fitted to stand the usual squalls of the climate, and, at that time, the only keeled boat on the Lake. When the weather did not allow of their excursions after dinner,--an occurrence not unfrequent during this very wet summer,--the inmates of the cottage passed their evenings at Diodati, and, when the rain rendered it inconvenient for them to return home, remained there to sleep. 'We often,' says one, who was not the least ornamental of the party [ie, Mary], 'sat up in conversation till the morning light. There was never any lack of subjects, and, grave or gay, we were always interested.'

This description gives an impression of the pleasure they must have found in one another's company. They became attached by bonds of real affection, even though they may seem an oddly assorted group: Shelley, intense, his imagination working overtime; Mary, thoughtful and calm; Claire, flitting up the path to the Villa at all hours; Dr Polidori, an often comic figure made sly fun of by the others; and Byron, the oldest of the group (at 28) sitting on his balcony thinking morosely of his late disgrace when not boating on the lake or laughing with the others. They were, of course, with their scandalous reputations for irregular sexual behavior, objects of curiosity. The proprietor of the Hotel d'Angleterre hired out telescopes to his English guests so that they could spy on Byron and his friends at the Villa Diodati across the lake. It was rumored that the curious could see "certain robes and flounces on his Lordship's balcony," presumed to be female underclothes belonging to Byron's mistresses, though probably household linen put out to dry. What Moore's description fails to mention is the productivity of the poets at this time. During this summer Shelley completed *Mt Blanc* and the *Hymn to Intellectual Beauty* and Byron wrote *Prometheus*, the

Third Canto of *Childe Harold* and a number of shorter poems. It was not all play.

*   *   *

Some of Byron's shorter pieces written that summer expressed his remorse and rancor at the breakdown of his marriage and his exile. Some were verses of love and longing addressed to Augusta. Also on his mind was his childhood love, Mary Chaworth.

In 1803 Byron's mother had written distractedly that she could not get Byron to return to Harrow because he was suffering from "love desperate, love the *worst of all maladies* in my opinion." Byron was then fifteen. Mary, the object of his affections, was eighteen. She was a distant cousin and a descendant of a man notoriously murdered by the Fifth Lord Byron--his great-uncle had killed hers. She was reputedly pretty, slim and with light brown hair, and the attraction was mutual, but there was no way the two could have married. Apart from the obstacle presented by the ancient enmity between the Byron and Chaworth families, Mary was already engaged to John Musters, a local squire. The marriage was a disaster. Musters was boorish and violent as well as unfaithful-- taking up "all kinds of vulgar mistresses," according to Byron-- and they separated.

Mary wrote to Byron in 1814 asking to meet him. The timing was awkward. Byron was involved with Augusta and about to marry Annabella. Augusta persuaded him not to see Mary. "If you go," Augusta advised, "you will fall in love again, and then there will be a scene; one step will lead to another, *et cela fera un éclat*." It was too late for both of them. Mary fell into mental and physical decline, ("You would hardly recognize in me the happy creature you once knew me," she wrote, "I am grown so thin, pale and gloomy.") Eventually she became insane. And yet, in the summer of 1816 Byron was mining the memory of this early love for inspiration, particularly in *The Dream* in which he uses his and Mary's story

for a tale of doomed lovers, "...two beings in the hues of youth /
Standing upon a hill..."

I was strangely touched to read, in some biographical notes Byron
wrote in 1821, a description of an episode he remembered when he
and Mary were in a boat together:

> When I was fifteen years of age, it happened that in a
> Cavern in Derbyshire I had to cross in a boat (in which
> two people only could lie down) a stream which flows
> under a rock with the rock so close upon the water as
> to admit the boat only to be pushed on by a ferry-man
> (a sort of Charon), who wades at the stern stooping
> all the time. The Companion of my transit was [Mary
> Chaworth] with whom I had been long in love, and
> never told it, though *she* had discovered it without. I
> recollect my sensations, but cannot describe them--and
> it is as well.

Reading this note brought back with uncanny clarity an experience
when I was about the age of Byron when he was in the boat with
Mary, or perhaps I was a bit younger. It was in Italy, on the Island
of Capri, at the famous Blue Grotto. We had met a Turkish family
and I had become fond of the daughter--I think her name was
Guner. The girl and I were separated from the others and put
together in a narrow boat to enter the sea cave, propelled from
the stern by another Charon-like boatman. I remember Guner
had dark hair with an auburn tint, curly, not hanging in ringlets
but gathered and secured behind her head. Her eyes were green
and she had an illuminating smile. Her skin was very fair. (I like
to imagine now that she was descended from some Circassian
slave or a boy taken from a Dalmatian village by the Ottomans in
one of their regular child-harvests, to be trained at the Porte for
service in the Sultan's household; but, of course, of this I know
nothing.) At the entrance to the Grotto the opening was quite
narrow and the rock was, as in Byron's Derbyshire cavern, close

upon the water. The Grotto itself, though, was spacious. The blue light seemed to blaze from the water and rippled aqueously on the walls. Guner, in a lustral gesture, dipped her hand in the water. Raising her arm and bending her pale elbow, her hand loosely suspended from the curve of her arm in a graceful arc, she let the shining drops fall upon her head and then, smiling as it were in benediction, onto mine.

* * *

Much of their time, that summer, when Shelley and Byron were not working, was spent on the lake. In 1821 Byron remembered that "Shelley was on the Lake much oftener than I, at all hours of the night and day; he almost lived on it..." Mary, in a letter, noted contentedly that the waves of the lake did not give her the usual sea-sickness, but, on the contrary, "the tossing of our boat raises my spirits and inspires me with unusual hilarity." Byron, too, caught the pleasure of evening excursions on the lake when the weather was benign. On these outings on "clear, placid Leman," the boat's sail was "as a noiseless wing," flowers gave off a "living fragrance from the shore" and on the ear "Drops the light drip of the suspended oar, / Or chirps the grasshopper one good-night more."

While they may have enjoyed a few placid evenings like this, the weather was very bad that summer. In the previous year great eruptions at Tambora in the Pacific had thrown a cloud of volcanic ash into the upper atmosphere, obscuring the sun and bringing heavy rain. Mary, in a letter, complained of "almost perpetual rain" but rejoiced at the thunder storms, "grander and more terrific" than any she had ever seen. "We watch them as they approach from the opposite side of the lake, observing the lightning play among the clouds in various parts of the heavens, and dart in jagged figures upon the piny heights of Jura, dark with the shadow of the overhanging cloud." One night she "enjoyed" a memorably fine storm. "The lake was lit up--the pines on Jura made visible, and all the scene illuminated for an instant, when a pitchy blackness succeeded, and the thunder came in frightful bursts over our heads amid the darkness." This almost reads like scene-setting for a film version of her novel *Frankenstein*. Byron, too, described these storms in the Third Canto of *Childe Harold*:

> How the lit lake shines, a phosphoric sea,
> And the big rain comes dancing to the earth!
> And now again 'tis black--and now, the glee
> Of the loud hills shakes with its mountain-mirth,
> As if they did rejoice o'er a young earthquake's birth.

More conspicuous even than the rain was the darkness. Byron's poem, *Darkness*, also written that summer, evokes these unusual weather conditions in a nightmare vision of a dying world where the "bright sun was extinguish'd."

It seems inevitable that, gathered at Diodati late at night, the talk should turn to stories of the eerie and fantastic. Byron read some verses from Coleridge's poem *Christabel,* a poem Byron greatly admired. He had heard Sir Walter Scott reciting it from memory the previous year. Byron thought it "the wildest and finest I ever heard in that kind of composition." In gratitude for this praise Coleridge sent Byron a copy of the poem, one of the only two copies then in existence, and Byron sent it to Murray urging him to publish it. Coleridge met Byron in London in April, just a few days before Byron left England, and recited his *Kubla Khan*-- then, like *Christabel*, both unfinished and unpublished. On Byron's recommendation Murray agreed to publish both poems and they appeared in print in May 1816, a few weeks before the reading at Diodati.

The poem concerns a witch who appears at first as a beautiful princess but who is in reality a lamia, a disguised serpent intent on the possession of the young girl, Christabel. The witch is put up in

Christabel's bed chamber. She casts a spell on Christabel and, while Christabel is in a half comatose state, undresses:

> Her silken robe, and inner Vest
> Dropt to her feet, and in full view,
> Behold! her bosom and half her side--
> Hideous, deformed and pale of hue--
> O shield her! Shield sweet Christabel!

In a state of terror Shelley ran shrieking from the room. Polidori threw some water in his face and gave him some ether to calm him. Shelley had been horrified by the vision of a woman who had eyes instead of nipples. Polidori sat up with Shelley while the others, exhausted, went to bed.

It is unclear why Shelley reacted as he did. Coleridge's description of the lamia's breasts was presumably meant to suggest her transformation into a serpent. Did Shelley's vision somehow reflect a bad conscience--that whenever he made love to Mary he was haunted by Harriet's accusing stare? Nothing elsewhere suggests he then felt guilt at his desertion of Harriet, but it is a possibility.

It may also be, less obviously, that Shelley's outburst was simply an explosion of the tensions of that summer during which he was undergoing a transformation of his awareness of the supernatural. He had often found himself beset by visions and pursued by spectres, or pursuing them ("While yet a boy I sought for ghosts...") Now these visions were giving way to a new and more philosophical awareness, which we might call religious in feeling, despite his protestations of atheism. In the *Hymn to Intellectual Beauty* his instinct for the noumenal found its outlet in the discovery of that universal spirit of beauty and love that would free the world from its "dark slavery". In *Mt Blanc*, also written that summer, the mountain is seen as the dwelling place of eternal power, "Remote, serene and inaccessible," the power which exhibits itself through time and change, the "secret strength of things." In these poems Shelley's imagination achieves a mystical identification of a supernatural power that animates all life, the ultimate unity of all being, quite different from his youthful ghosts or the tormenting visions of the kind he had at Diodati.

*   *   *

One evening Byron proposed a kind of competition. Each of the party should compose a ghost story. Byron's contribution was a story later printed at the end of his *Mazeppa*. Polidori came up with *The Vampyre* which was published in 1819. Mary at first could not think of anything, but a few days later a discussion between Byron and Shelley on "the nature of the principle of life", prompted by reports of the galvanic experiments that were popular at the time, gave her the germ of an idea. Encouraged by Byron she set to work. Her production, *Frankenstein*, is now certainly the most widely known product of that fertile summer.

It is also likely that the myth of Prometheus was the subject of some of their late night discussions. The wild weather and mountain scenery may have inspired it. Both Byron and Shelley had read Aeschylus' *Prometheus Bound*. Byron made a translation of part of it when he was at Harrow and this was included in his first published collection of verse, *Hours of Idleness*. For him, he wrote, the myth had "always been so much in my head that I can easily conceive its influence over all or anything I have written." Byron composed his *Prometheus* that summer. When *Frankenstein* was published it was sub-titled *A Modern Prometheus*. Shelley's re-working of the myth was written two years later, but for him too the mountain scenery was evocative. Crossing the Alps in 1818 on his way to Italy he found a "scene...like that described in the Prometheus of Aeschylus; vast rifts and caverns in the granite precipices; wintry mountains with ice and snow above; the loud sounds of unseen waters within the caverns; and walls of toppling rocks..."

The treatments of the Prometheus story, as found in Aeschylus, by Byron, Mary and Shelley were each very different. As told by Aeschylus, Zeus, in the struggle between the Gods and the Titans, overthrew his father, Kronos, and seized for himself supreme power over heaven and earth. The Titan Prometheus, who had sided with Zeus in the struggle, incurred the wrath of Zeus. Zeus had planned to destroy the human race and create another. Prometheus, out of pity, stole fire from heaven and brought it to mankind. As a punishment, Zeus had Prometheus bound to a rock in the Caucasus; each day his liver was to be torn out by a vulture, to be healed anew for the next day's torment. But Prometheus has the knowledge which, if told to Zeus, could set him free, and which he will not reveal. That is the secret of how Zeus himself will be overthrown--by his progeny. Buried in this story is the primitive fear of fathers, that their sons will supplant them; as in the companion myth in which Zeus had to restrain his desire for Thetis because of the prophecy that she would give birth to a son stronger than his father.

Byron's youthful translation of Aeschylus contains, in sharp contrast to his later treatment of the subject, lines indicating the suffering Titan's silent submission to almighty Jove (Zeus): "My voice shall raise no impious strain / 'Gainst him who rules the sky and azure main." Prometheus must yield to necessity. But the Prometheus Byron created in the summer of 1816 was all proud defiance in spite of defeat and suffering and loneliness. This more closely matched Byron's then mood in the face of loss and rejection. The Titan's suffering ("The rock, the vulture and the chain / All that the proud can feel of pain"), his endurance of the torments inflicted by vindictive Hate, are seen as a "mighty lesson" to mortals, teaching them to endure and face with stoicism their "unallied existence." In this Prometheus is like other Byronic heroes, Manfred for instance, whose defiance is rooted in their proud autonomy and who are raised above nature, fate or the gods by their indomitable will. They may face ceaseless struggle, but their integrity is preserved. This was the Romantic idea of heroic authenticity, where the readiness to suffer for a principle counts for more than the validity of the principle itself. In the words of Isaiah Berlin, "if the revolt of Prometheus against the Olympian gods doomed him to eternal torment, then so much the worse for Olympus."

Mary copied this poem for Byron and carried it to Murray when she returned to England at the end of the summer. But, though she admired it, she seems in her novel to have been influenced more by Aeschylus' original play than by Byron's poem to the extent that the emphasis is more on the gift to man which Prometheus stole from heaven than on Prometheus' suffering and defiance. Aeschylus makes clear that the fire which Prometheus brought to man, inaugurating human civilization, was an ambiguous gift. Encompassed within it is all of human imagination and intelligence. It brings blind hope to men so that they "might cease to live with death in sight." Even more, it brought the power to think: "through me they won their minds," and thus all human culture, arts, letters and science and "the mother of all arts, hard working memory." [Edith Hamilton translation.] Fire, in this sense, includes all that Claude Levi-Strauss suggested in his distinction between the raw and the cooked, the distinction between nature and culture, the separation of what is free from human control from what humans organize and domesticate. What Mary caught hold of in her novel is the impiety of the gift, a theft which enables man to defy the Gods and violate divine order. This is the crime of Dr Frankenstein as Prometheus for which he is condemned not to be chained to a rock but to pursue his creature across the frozen wastes, a setting inspired by Mary's visit to a Swiss glacier, the *mer de glace*. There is also the muted suggestion that Frankenstein, in his blind idealism, shows some of the emotional narcissism of Shelley himself; a romantic idealism which masks selfishness and indifference to the feelings of others. Here may lurk a premonition of feelings which came to Mary later, even if they were not evident in 1816.

By the time Shelley took up the Prometheus theme three years had passed. But in some ways his *Prometheus Unbound* is a continuation of a three-way conversation about the myth and its meaning, a conversation which began in the summer of 1816. For Shelley, Aeschylus' play held the promise that mankind might be freed, like Prometheus, from the tyranny of Zeus--with which he would, doubtless, identify the political tyrannies of his time. Aeschylus' Prometheus held the knowledge which, if he imparted it to Zeus, could free him. This is the knowledge of who would, in time, overthrow Zeus--it will be Zeus' own offspring out of Io. Prometheus refuses to give up the secret. He bears his torment in the confident knowledge that Zeus has "his little moment of lording it in heaven" and will finally be overthrown. "So let him sit enthroned in confidence, trust to his crushing thunder high in air, shake in his hands his fire-breathing dart. Surely these shall be no defense, but he will fall in shame unbearable. Even now he makes ready against himself one who shall wrestle with him and prevail, a wonder of wonders..." [Edith Hamilton, again.] With this prediction Prometheus' final plea is for justice: "O holy mother Earth, O air and sun, behold me, I am wronged..."

It is easy to see how Shelley, with his utopian and revolutionary ideas, would respond to this aspect of Aeschylus' play. Unfortunately, the sequel which Aeschylus wrote, in which Prometheus and Zeus are reconciled, is now lost; but Shelley devised an original resolution in his *Prometheus Unbound*, with the invention of two new characters, Asia and Demogorgon. Asia, the principle of eternal love, visits Demogorgon, the destined child of Jupiter (Zeus) in his lair outside the physical world. Demogorgon, who seems to be a spirit of all energy and wisdom, encouraged by Asia, ascends to heaven, deposes Jupiter and retires. Prometheus is unbound by Hercules and united with Asia. At the heart of the poem, which is lengthy and complex, is Shelley's optimistic faith that, given love and good will, human failings were eradicable. His reading of Godwin-- and Rousseau--convinced him of the essential goodness of man if released from the burdens and deformations imposed by tyranny and stale custom. Shelley also brings his Platonism into line with Godwinian utopianism, seeing the evil and injustice apparent in the world as a superficial blemish which cannot efface the eternal truth. Shelley's great poem can then be seen as a kind of riposte to the interpretations of the myth put forward by both Byron and Mary. For Byron, man, like Prometheus, has no alternative to suffering other than endurance and proud defiance. Mary suggests that Promethean man, in his arrogance, lacks the moral capacity to handle the fire stolen from heaven. For Shelley, Prometheus could overcome the curse of Jupiter and replace fate--and hate--through the power of liberating love.

This idea of love as an intervening daemon owed much to Shelley's reading of Plato, and particularly *The Symposium* (*The Banquet* in Shelley's version) which he translated while living near Bagni di Lucca during the summer of 1818. In the Diotima colloquy Love is described as neither a god nor a mortal but something intermediate. Old Horace, in the Ode misquoted by Byron in his letter to Hobhouse in June 1811, attributes the torments of love to the intervention of the god against which he is helpless despite his age ("Intermissa, Venus, diu rursus bella moves?") He urges her to go away and torment someone younger. The pains or joys of love are in the power of the god to bestow (or inflict) as the god chooses. Diotima, however, sees Love as a daemon, neither human nor divine, but making possible communication between the two-- "all that intercourse and converse which is conceded by the Gods to men, both whilst they sleep and when they wake, subsists through the intervention of Love…" (Shelley's translation).

Most of us encounter at some time love as imagined by Horace and by Diotima: that is, love which seems to come unbidden as from an outside source, bringing unasked for and unexpected pleasure (and pain); and love which seems to come as an inner illumination, a (generally) joyful epiphany revealing a world full of so much greater promise than any we can imagine in our normal, sober, moments.

*   *   *

45

On June 22nd Shelley and Byron set off together on a boat trip around the lake. Polidori, to Byron's relief, was unable to come with them. Polidori had taken a fancy to Mary. Seeing her approach along the path, Byron teased Polidori, who was then on the balcony of the Villa, saying that if he were a gentleman he would jump down to offer her his arm. Polidori did so and sprained his ankle. So the two poets set off alone except for two boatmen to help them manage the boat. The voyage took eight days.

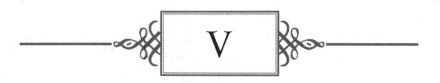

Savoy - Meillerie - Rhone - Chillon

I returned to my hotel in Geneva. The following morning I walked to the quai and got on the steamer for Vevey. The course of my journey followed almost precisely that taken by Byron and Shelley, starting off along the Savoy shore and crossing the lake near Meillerie. The events of their voyage are recorded in Byron's correspondence and in a long letter from Shelley to Thomas Love Peacock dated July 12, 1816.

Byron and Shelley set off, with their boatmen rowing, at half past two. The lake was calm. By the evening they had arrived at the village of Nernier. In his letter to Peacock Shelley mentions an encounter there. After a walk along the lakeside, the lake a beautiful expanse of "purple and misty waters" broken by craggy islets near the shore, Shelley and Byron sat on a wall and observed some children playing a game. These children appeared "in an extraordinary way deformed and diseased." Most of them were "crooked" and with enlarged throats, obviously suffering from some goitrous condition. But one little boy was of an exquisite gracefulness and beauty. Shelley noted that "There was a mixture of pride and gentleness in his eyes and lips, the indications of sensibility, which his education will probably pervert to misery or seduce to crime..." However it did seem that the boy's "original wildness" might have been tamed by the "habitual exercise of milder feelings." Byron gave the boy some money which he took without speaking and with "a sweet smile of easy thankfulness." The reality of life here might be harsh and brutal, Shelley thinks, but his imagination gives it a rosier tint on this "serene and glowing evening, in this remote and romantic village, beside the calm lake..."

When my steamer pulled up to the dock at Nernier there were a number of children there, none of them diseased or deformed. Houses built of stone crowd around the small port. Originally fishermen's cottages, they are now modernized and restored but one can imagine the poverty that once lurked in these crowded dwellings.

From Nernier the steamer passes close to the shore. A dark wood lies between Nernier and the next village, Yvoire, which is as Shelley described it, "a scattered village with an ancient castle, whose houses are interspersed with trees". Not quite so scattered, to be sure. There has been a certain amount of infilling over the last century. The village church has a strange-shaped spire, with a silvery shine, its bulbous shape mimicking not so much an onion as a turnip or even a radish. Yvoire, at the narrowest point of the crescent-shaped lake, is now a popular holiday destination for the French and a number of tourists were crowding the dock. Despite this bustle there seemed to me to be something oppressive about the French side of the lake. The mountains seemed to loom overhead. The houses were grayer and more compressed. There were no spacious villas or chateaux as on the Swiss side. Shelley noted this too, though for him the gloom translated as an "aspect of wilder magnificence." He observed with delight that "The mountains of Savoy, whose summits were bright with snow, descended in broken slopes to the lake; on high, the rocks were dark with pine forests, which became deeper and more immense, until the ice and snow mingle with the points of naked rock that pierce the blue air; but below, groves of walnut, chestnut and oak, with openings of lawny fields, attested the milder climate."

Perhaps it was just the change in the weather that made this side of the lake seem oppressive to me. Grey clouds were rolling across the sky and it began to rain. The lake surface was smooth but took on the sheen of polished pewter. Crossing the lake it got darker, though on the western horizon a gleam of light hovered over the water. Lake currents made feathery patterns on the surface. At the edge of the lake the darkness was punctured by flashes, the warning lights at the end of the dock at each harbor. An hour later it began to rain harder, and steadily.

This weather was beginning to resemble in inclemency that encountered by Shelley and Byron, though it was not so violent or changeable. On June 24th Shelley reported "more rapid changes of atmosphere than I ever recollect to have observed before. The morning was cold and wet; then an easterly wind and the clouds hard and high; then thunder showers, and wind shifting to every quarter; then a warm blast from the south, and summer clouds hanging over the peaks, with bright blue sky between." There were, later, flashes of lightning from a dark cloud directly overhead prompting a reference to Horace's description of lightning-wielding Jupiter.

The weather got worse the next day, with a violent wind and high waves. Off the rocks at Meillerie there was a near disaster. Shelley described it thus: "...the wind gradually increased in violence, until it blew tremendously; and, as it came from the remotest extremity of the lake, produced waves of a frightful height, and covered the whole surface with a chaos of foam. One of our boatmen, who was a dreadfully stupid fellow, persisted in holding the sail at a time when the boat [which Byron elsewhere described as being small and overloaded] was on the point of being driven under water by the hurricane. On discovering his error, he let it entirely go and the boat for a moment refused to obey the helm; in addition, the rudder was so broken as to render the management of it very difficult; one wave fell in, and then another. My companion [Byron], an excellent swimmer, took off his coat, I did the same, and we sat with our arms crossed, every instant expecting to be swamped." But in a short while they managed to get control of the boat and, despite the high waves, got to safety at the village of St Gingolph, where Byron noted that the tempest had blown down some "fine old chestnut trees". On June 27th Byron wrote to John Murray and referred to the squall and the near wreck. "I ran no risk," he wrote, "being so near the rocks, and a good swimmer; but our party were wet, and incommoded a good deal..." What neither Shelley nor Byron mentions in these accounts is that Shelley could not swim, though Shelley admits in his letter that he had felt the nearness of death by drowning. "I felt in this near prospect of death a mixture of sensations, among which terror entered, though but subordinately. My feelings would have been less painful had I been alone; but I knew that my companion would have attempted to save me, and I was overcome with humiliation, when I thought that his life might have been risked to preserve mine." Byron later would bear witness to Shelley's courage and resignation. He was "as cool as it was possible to be in such circumstances." Shelley said that he "had no notion of being saved," and that Byron would have enough to do to save himself without trying to save his friend. As Byron wrote of Shelley then: "he don't want courage."

Reading this it is hard not to think of the scene on the beach near Livorno six years later, in July 1822, and Shelley's drowned corpse, identified by the copy of Keats' poems in the jacket pocket, and the arrangements to burn the body made by Edward Trelawny. While Trelawny was at this business with the iron rack on which the bodies were burned Byron swam far out to sea. While swimming, whether from exhaustion or revulsion, Byron vomited in the water. As the body was consumed Byron tried to retrieve the skull, which fell to pieces in the flames. Only Trelawny claimed a relic, Shelley's heart which he snatched up when Shelley's breast burst open. The heart, exuding a viscous liquid, had failed to burn. It was taken, preserved in wine, then dried. The inscription on the monument over Shelley's ashes at the Protestant Cemetery in Rome ("COR CORDIUM") is misleading. The only fragment of his remains not there is his heart. After being claimed for a while by Leigh Hunt, it was given to Mary and turned up on her death in a desk drawer wrapped in a copy of *Adonais*. It was finally laid in the Shelley family vault at Bournemouth, probably the last place Shelley would have wanted to hold any of his remains.

It is too fanciful to see in this episode on the lake a sort of dress rehearsal of Shelley's end, but it is remarkable how often Shelley was drawn to water and thoughts of drowning. Trelawny tells of how Shelley once plunged into a deep pool and lay motionless, like a fish, on the bottom until he was pulled out by his friends. Trelawny is unreliable, but it is still noticeable how Shelley came to be haunted by images of the sea and death. His verse is full of references to shipwreck and drowning. Frequently this is described in some of his most vivid and immediate language, as in the closing line of his *Ode to Liberty* describing "waves which lately paved his watery way" now "Hiss round a drowner's head in their tempestuous play." Nowhere is this more specific than in the Stanzas written in Naples in 1818. Sitting on the beach alone the "lightning of the noon-tide ocean" flashing around him, he reflects that he has "nor health nor peace within...Nor fame, nor power, nor love, nor leisure." In this despair he could "lie down like a tired child / And weep away the the life of care

> Till death like sleep might steal on me,
> And I might feel in the warm air
> My cheek grow cold, and hear the sea
> Breathe o'er my dying brain its last monotony..."

At the end of *Adonais* Shelley would write, a year before his own death, of his soul sailing out to meet the beckoning soul of the dead Keats: "my spirit's bark is driven far from the shore."

In his last strange days at the Casa Magni near Lerici he took Jane Williams out in a small boat and seemed, as she reported, to be contemplating a suicide pact, that they should drown together. When Shelley's boat, the *Ariel* (originally christened the *Don Juan* by Byron and Trelawny), went down in that fatal squall one of the sailors in sight of it reported that someone on the boat (probably Edward Williams, Shelley's companion) was trying to lower sail but was being resisted by another. Was this Shelley, intent on driving the boat into the storm-tossed sea?

* * *

After this near drowning in the lake Shelley and Byron took a carriage to pass the Rhone where it enters the lake. Shelley described passing between the mountains and the lake "under groves of mighty chesnut [sic] trees, beside perpetual streams, which are nourished by the snows above and form stalactites on the rocks, over which they fall." Some of the trees had been knocked down in the recent storm. Where the Rhone joined it the lake was "marked by a line of tremendous breakers", the river being "as rapid as when it leaves the lake" (at Geneva), but "muddy and dark."

This place now bears little resemblance to the scene described by Shelley. At the end of the 19th century the river was tamed, canalized, and most of the marsh at the entrance to the lake turned into agricultural land. A little of the marsh remains in the nature reserve of Les Grangettes where footpaths lead by the lake among marsh reeds and through some thick woodland. There are grebes, many kinds of duck, mergansers, cormorants. Drainage channels cross the marsh and the lake edge is brown with runoff. This is all that remains of Shelley's "willowy plain of the Rhone."

On the day I walked there the skies were dark. As I reached the Grand Canal--all that is left of the mighty Rhone at this point--the late summer rain came on heavily. Apart from the sound of the falling rain all was silent. The holiday cottages were deserted. A heron stood resignedly by the river, if river is the right term for the canal following a straight course from as far as I could see in the mist. The waters rushed, celadon green, beneath a bridge. Turning in the direction of the lake I saw a dredger beginning to work where the ditch, which was once a mighty river, emptied itself into the lake.

As I retreated from this remnant of the Rhone, the rain fell even harder. On the path, in the gloom, some distance away, appeared a figure at first resembling a double of myself. As I drew closer to this *doppelganger* he resolved himself into a man walking his dog, the only living creatures, apart from myself, in this sodden, desolate, landscape. We walked together in near silence to his car, which he had left a quarter of a mile away, and he gave me a lift to the village of Villeneuve where I caught the bus to Vevey.

*   *   *

Passing the Rhone ("rapid even at a great distance from its confluence with the lake") Shelley and Byron proceeded to the Chateau de Chillon, a visit which was to be fruitful, in a literary sense, for Byron, whose poem invokes the prisoner in the sinister dungeons. How familiar to us all is the view of that stumpy fortress moored, miraculously, in the lake! I must have come to that castle for the first time in childhood with my parents and sister. Seeing it again, its familiar bulk seeming to float upon the water, it was to me as yesterday. Shelley, too, felt something of the same. In his letter to Peacock he refers to the chateau, along with Clarens and the mountains of the Valais, as "present[ing] themselves to the imagination as monuments to things that were once familiar, and of beings that were once dear to it." For him it was the power of Rousseau's Julie rather than childhood memories that bore the burden of nostalgia, but the phenomenon was much the same.

On the more recent occasion, as if by a miracle, the clouds, which had hovered over the lake all morning parted. Suddenly the water gleamed and the hills bloomed with velvety green. Even Meillerie on the Savoy shore came into view. The sun fell in broad shafts through gaps in the clouds disclosing shreds of blue sky. The lake, now emerald, was ruffled by white caps which chased a *vapeur* ("La Suisse") of the kind with thrashing side paddle wheels driven by gleaming pistons-- still going strong after a century. This, along with the castle walls themselves, so often lending themselves as subjects for artists of every quality, reinforced my sense that the view was changeless. Even this nautical artifact seemed to me an aspect of nature, its blasts as fitting as the whistles of the lake birds.

At the castle itself it was less the lake view than the gloom and horror of the dungeons that struck Shelley and Byron; and that, it must be admitted, also left its impress on my youthful imagination. On the columns of the dungeon, Shelley observed, were "engraven a multitude of names, partly those of visitors, and partly doubtless of the prisoners, of whom now no memory remains, and who thus beguiled a solitude which they have long ceased to feel." Even in 1816 I suspect the names of tourists outnumbered those of prisoners, and by now most of the names carved there (I noted Branson, Cox, Barlow, Hall) seem more likely to be those of English and American "visitors" than victims of ancient tyranny and religious persecution. Byron, famously, added his own name, and there it was, just as I remembered it, framed behind a piece of glass. I recalled my mother remarking that if it had been any name but Byron's it would be condemned as an act of vandalism, not framed like a holy relic.

Despite the apparent timelessness of the view of the castle and the lake, as I turned aside to walk to the landing stage for the boat back to Vevey I saw that the hand of man has not been idle since the time of the visit of Shelley and Byron and even that of my young self. The buildings of Montreux now come almost to the walls of the castle and a motorway on stilts is wrapped like a chaplet around the wooded hill behind.

Clarens and Rousseau

Clarens, with its associations with Rousseau and his heroine Julie, was in some ways, for Shelley, the object of the entire trip. He took with him a copy of *Julie, ou la Nouvelle Héloise*. He had not read it before, though Mary read it at the beginning of the summer. It is, perhaps, surprising he had not read it. When Godwin was courting Mary Wollstonecraft she said she wanted a "bird's eye view" of his heart and, as a kind of test of his capacity for feeling, accompanied her letter with one of her favorite books, *Julie*. Now Shelley was visiting the scenes of the novel with the book in hand. As Shelley wrote in his letter to Peacock, it was there that he "first knew the divine beauty of Rousseau's imagination, as it exhibits itself in Julie." Visiting the places where the action of the novel took place added greatly to its effect. "It is inconceivable what an enchantment the scene itself lends to those delineations, from which its own most touching charm arises." Byron, too, was responsive to Rousseau. In the Third Canto of *Childe Harold* he hailed Rousseau ("One, whose dust was once all fire") as a "self-tormenting sophist" who threw "Enchantment over passion." It was Rousseau's passion for ideal beauty which "breathed itself to life in Julie." In a footnote to his poem he made the connection between the scenery and the novel in words which echo Shelley: "It would be difficult to see Clarens (with the scenes around it...) without being forcibly struck with its peculiar adaptation to the persons and events with which it has been peopled." He goes further. The feelings with which these scenes are invested "is of a still higher and more comprehensive order than the mere sympathy with individual passion; it is a sense of the existence of love at its most extended and sublime capacity, and of our own participation of its good and of its glory; it is the great principle of the universe, which is there more condensed, but not less manifested; and of which, though knowing ourselves a part, we lose our individuality, and mingle in the beauty of the whole- -If Rousseau had never written, nor lived, the same associations would not less have belonged to such scenes..." Love and scenery here combined to provide a means to a transcendental experience.

This interest in and appreciation of Rousseau's *Julie* shown by Shelley and Byron was the latest development in the fluctuating reputation of the novel among English readers. When *Julie* first appeared in England in 1761 it became something of a best seller, treated as a novel of sentiment like Richardson's *Pamela*. There was also a widespread sympathy for the ideas of Rousseau which were seen as an attack on urban decadence and luxury, contrasting it with a (Swiss) rural life which was the antithesis of Parisian sophistication. When James Boswell made his pilgrimage to Rousseau at his refuge at Motiers in 1764 he sought him as a man of true sensibility, the man of sentiment living the simple retired life. Boswell was careful to introduce himself as a "man with a feeling heart." Notwithstanding the condemnation of *Emile* as heretical by the Parlement of Paris because of the faith of the Savoyard vicar therein expressed (which was only an expression of simplistic piety), Rousseau was welcomed in England when he came in 1766. By then Rousseau's quarrelsomeness and paranoia, quite apart from his supposed heresy, had made him unpopular in every circle on the continent. He lost little time in alienating his English friends. Even Boswell cooled, remarking in 1768 that it had been better for Rousseau to have remained in the romantic retirement where he had found him four years before: "When he was at a distance, his singular eloquence filled our minds with high ideas of the wild philosopher. When he came into the walks of men we knew, alas! how much these ideas suffered."

It was not, however, Rousseau's generally rebarbative personality nor his philosophical or religious ideas which turned the English reading public against him, but two events which occurred after Rousseau died in 1778. The first was the posthumous publication of Rousseau's *Confessions* which, because of the revelations of the author's sometimes disreputable early experiences, repelled English reviewers. Rousseau was condemned as both vain and immoral. Even Mary Wollstonecraft, an admirer of *Julie*, had to warn her readers against what she saw as the scandalous sensuality of the *Confessions*.

The second event which counted against Rousseau was the French Revolution. The enthusiasm of Robespierre and the National Convention for Rousseau, and the transfer of his corpse from Ermenonville to the Pantheon, lent credence to the claim that he was somehow responsible for the Revolution and the Terror which followed. In this respect he was lumped together with the *philosophes* who had been his enemies while he lived and with whom he had little in common. Edmund Burke launched a savage attack in 1791. Interestingly, he does not attack Rousseau as a political theorist (he does not mention the *Social Contract*, though Rousseau's blueprint for a totalitarian republic would have appealed to Robespierre) but as a moralist. Rousseau, he alleges, led the revolutionaries in their attack on traditional values, not just political arrangements but attitudes and manners, particularly attitudes to love and sex. So the novel *Julie* assumes a central place in Burke's attack. The revolutionaries, according to Burke, have found the attitudes given voice in the novel convenient to their goals of undermining society. "Through him they teach men to love after the fashion of philosophers..an unfashioned, indelicate, sour, gloomy, ferocious medley of pedantry and lewdness--of metaphysical speculations blended with the coarsest sensuality. Such is the general morality of the passions to be found in their famous philosopher, in his famous work of philosophic gallantry, the *Nouvelle Héloise*." Rousseau is an erotic leveler, useful to the revolutionaries in their task of destroying respectable society. In the advances of St Preux, the tutor, to his high-born pupil, Julie, Burke uncovers a plot to have menials seduce the aristocratic daughters of France, who will become "easy prey to dancing masters, fiddlers, pattern-drawers, friseurs and valets de chambre." Burke brings together the subversiveness of *Julie* and the salaciousness of the *Confessions*. This set the tone of criticism until the fall of Napoleon; repugnance at Rousseau's life as revealed in the *Confessions* enabled critics to scent a whiff of lust and immorality in *Julie*. When it first appeared *Julie* was seen as a masterpiece of sentiment. By 1805 that sentiment was widely seen as a mask for sensuality and subversion. Even Wordsworth and Coleridge saw Rousseau much as Burke saw him. But by 1815 the next generation of romantics saw him differently.

One of the new champions of Rousseau was William Hazlitt. His article, *On the Character of Rousseau*, appeared in Leigh Hunt's journal, *The Examiner*, of 14 April, 1816. While it appeared as Shelley and Byron were making ready to depart for the continent, I know of no evidence that either of them read it, though it is tempting to believe so. Hazlitt starts by condemning the opinion of Mme de Stael that Rousseau's principal quality was his strength of reason on abstract questions. Instead, Hazlitt writes: "The only quality which he possessed in an eminent degree, which alone raised him above ordinary men and which gave to his writings and opinions an influence greater, perhaps, than has been exerted by any individual in modern times, was extreme sensibility, or an acute and even morbid feeling of all that related to his own impressions, to the objects and events of his life. He had the most intense consciousness of his own existence. No object that had once made an impression on him was ever after effaced. Every feeling in his mind became a passion. His craving after excitement was an appetite and a disease. His interest in his own thoughts and feelings was always wound up to the highest pitch...His fictitious characters are modifications of his own being, reflections and shadows of himself." Rousseau's philosophical speculations are briskly dismissed by Hazlitt as the "obvious exaggerations of a mind giving loose to its habitual impulses and moulding all nature to its own purposes" which "involved him in endless wilful contradictions." Rousseau's "quarrel with the artificial institutions and distinctions of society" was only the outcome of this wayward personality, which "sought the unrestrained indulgence of his will, and allured his imagination to scenes of pastoral simplicity or of savage life, where the passions were either not excited or left to follow their own impulse-where the petty vexations and irritating disappointments of common life had no place--and where the tormenting pursuits of arts and sciences were lost in pure animal enjoyment, or indolent repose." Contrary to all then received opinion, Hazlitt pronounces the *Confessions* "the best of all his works"-- it "relates entirely to himself; and no one was ever so much at home on this subject as he was." Even so, due to their intensity, "he makes us enter into his feelings as if they had been our own and we seem to remember every incident and circumstance of his life as if it had happened to ourselves." To make his defense of Rousseau complete Hazlitt even has a stab at Burke (a man "half poet and half philosopher" who "has done more mischief than perhaps any other person in the world"), even alleging that his jealousy of Rousseau was the chief cause of his opposition to the French Revolution.

Hazlitt, in his review, expresses one of the features of the state of mind we have come to call Romantic, which is the emphasis on sincerity as an outstanding virtue, as observed in Byron's *Prometheus*. The conviction with which something is said, and its untempered honesty, now count almost as much as the value of the thing expressed. Related to this is the value placed on the sheer energy found even in Rousseau's uncompromising egotism. He was, according to Hazlitt, the "first who held the torch (lighted at the never-ending fire in his own bosom) to the hidden chambers in the mind of man..." He compares him to "another Prometheus" who "breathed into his nostrils the breath of a new and intellectual life, enraging the Gods of the earth..." This egotism became an eruptive force, which could not accept subordination. This was a conception of a particular self which dominated the romantic imagination--a personality which, through its penetrating creative energy, was a source of values.

59

Both Byron and Shelley could respond to this vision of Rousseau. For Byron, if Rousseau was a "wretched man" and the "apostle of affliction" he also threw "enchantment over passion" and knew how to "make madness beautiful." His love for ideal beauty as exhibited in *Julie* "teems / Along his burning page, distemper'd though it seems." If Rousseau is mad or perverse, then this is the price he paid for inspiration. The purest expression of this energy is the passionate but ideal eroticism of *Julie*.

For Shelley, reading *Julie* enabled him to see Rousseau not as a philosopher but as a visionary poet who celebrated the dominion of love. In his *Defence of Poetry* Shelley stated his creed thus: "The great secret of morals is love, or a going out of our own nature and an identification of ourselves with the beautiful which exists in thought, action, or person not our own. A man to be greatly good, must imagine intensely and comprehensively; he must put himself in the place of another and of many others; the pains and pleasures of his species must become his own. The great instrument of moral good is the imagination." Intensity of feeling, then, such as that expressed in *Julie*, became a moral imperative.

*   *   *

I sat down in my Vevey hotel with a translation of *Julie*. The resemblance to the story of Eloise and Abelard is superficial. It is about love in its various aspects, with a good deal of torment and twisted psychological analysis. Its epistolary form (like Richardson's novels) makes it seem artificial to a modern reader; and it is occasionally marred by pseudo-editorial comment, under Rousseau's own name, with didactic commentary, redundant information and irritating moral asides. Despite all that, it holds the attention of the reader.

St Preux is the tutor to Julie, the daughter of a Swiss nobleman, at the family estate at Clarens. In the first letter St Preux declares his love for Julie. He sees the hopelessness of his situation, since he could never be a simple seducer and his lowly station prevents their marriage. He describes Julie's charms in terms that, despite his ardor, seem a bit cool: her sweet disposition, her benevolence to the less fortunate, her exquisite taste and the purity of her soul. In desperation, he sees no choice but to leave. He asks Julie to send him away without further punishment. He bids her adieu.

Julie, in reply, sends short notes bidding St Preux to stay and in a long letter expresses her confusion. She loves St Preux, but sees her love as a horrible precipice to which she is running. Love is poisoning her sense and reason. She begs St Preux, in effect, to protect her from herself. St Preux, in reply, protests that he loves virtue even more than he loves Julie and, despite the agitation of his senses, will preserve her purity.

It is while the lovers are in this precarious state that Julie's cousin Claire enters the story. While the physical appearance of the girls is scarcely described it is shown that Julie is blonde and sweet and Claire is brunette and witty. Julie writes to Claire begging her to come to Clarens and stiffen Julie's resistance. Claire at once replies and tells Julie to be sensible. Does she really think that her father would allow Julie to marry a penniless bourgeois tutor? If not that, then what is she doing? Claire offers to come and be an eighteen-year-old duenna.

With Claire on the scene Julie becomes more tranquil, basking in St Preux's love while feeling herself innocent of any impropriety. St Preux, like any man, finds this situation intolerable. Juiie's ardent love has become too tranquil--and Claire is always present. For St Preux it is nearly impossible to continue to deny himself the physical fulfillment of his love--to keep the "rash pledge" he has given. As for Julie, who taunts St Preux for the speed with which he has become tired of being honorable, the anxiety and terror she felt when she first found herself falling in love has given way to a belief that she can love without losing her honor. Enjoying the pleasure of a guiltless passion in a union of love and innocence seems to her paradise on earth. Sex would destroy this.

St Preux, now, will have none of this. Who would prefer moderate happiness to bliss? He is tortured by desire. But Julie's response is only to praise him for his restraint, given his ardent spirit. She acknowledges their love, her belief that their destinies are forever united ("our souls touch at all points") despite the lack of physical intimacy. St Preux can only acquiesce. He turns again to his duties and writes that he is preparing a new plan of study for Julie and Claire--some light literature for Claire but heavier stuff for Julie.

It is at this point, with Julie avowedly determined on a chaste love and St Preux submissive, that Julie springs a surprise. St Preux, she writes, has a beautiful soul and can truly appreciate the delights of nature--particularly the grove near the house which will receive new value as the shelter of true, though chaste, lovers. She suggests they meet there under the arbor, with the "inseparable cousin" as chaperone. This is the scene of their first real embrace, the first passionate kiss. First St Preux grants Claire's request for a kiss—a kiss of pure friendship; but then, kissing Julie in her turn, he is immediately inflamed by sensual pleasure. Julie feels it too. She swoons and is supported by Claire. In his agitated letter St Preux pours forth: "your rosy lips...Julie's lips...pressed against mine and my body clasped in your arms...From our burning lips fire breathed forth with our sighs, and my heart was at the point of death under the weight of sensual pleasure."

St Preux now declares that he can no longer put up with abstinence and must, as he writes, die at Julie's feet or in her arms. Julie, alarmed by this heightening of intensity, sends St Preux away to the mountains for the summer, a cooling period. There he pines for Julie as Julie, at Clarens, pines for him. With the approach of winter Julie, concerned for his health and comfort in the snows, calls St Preux back. Besides, she feels that the weight of his absence is crushing her. Despite that, St Peux is not welcomed at Clarens. He takes refuge at Meillerie on the opposite shore of the lake, from the heights of which he could, tormentingly, see Julie's home. "What bitterness," he writes, "is mixed with the sweetness of coming home to you again...Oh Julie, what a fatal gift from heaven is a sensitive soul!" In a frenzy, and in freezing cold, St Preux dashes from crag to crag with a telescope hoping to catch a glimpse of Julie's window. Whatever reserve he had been able to summon up is no more. "Enthusiasm for chastity," he tells her, "takes away your reason, and your virtue is no more than a delirium." They have not world enough nor time. "Opportunity slips away. Your beauty, even your beauty, will have its end...Think, think, Julie that we are already counting years lost for pleasure. Think that they will never return...Oh my blind love! You are seeking an imaginary happiness for a future which we shall never have. You are intent upon a distant time, and you do not see that meanwhile we are continually wasting away, and that our souls, overwhelmed by love and sorrow, are melting like the snow. Awake, there is still time... Come. oh my soul, into your lover's arms to reunite the two halves of our single being."

This unanswerable argument was enough to bring Julie to nervous breakdown. She takes to her bed and is, according to Claire, at the brink of death. It is sensible Claire, then, seeing Julie in such distress, who hires the boat to bring St Preux across the lake to his lover.

The consummation of their love leaves Julie with misgivings. Could she elope with St Preux? This would distress her father and "plunge a dagger" into her mother's heart. She feels remorse on her own account too. "I forgot everything but love," she writes to Claire. "One unguarded moment has ruined me forever. I have fallen into the abyss of shame from which a girl never returns..." Claire, always practical, provides reassurance, urging Julie not to distress herself unduly. "Is true love degrading to the soul?" she asks rhetorically. Better to love truly and keep the affair silent. St Preux also deplores Julie's self-chastisement and is humiliated by this show of repentance. Has not Julie obeyed "the purest laws of nature" in giving herself to the man she loves?

While, for Julie, having lost her innocence, the "sweet enchantment of virtue is vanished like a dream," she soon becomes more comfortable with the situation. In the way of fallen, or married, women she becomes almost domestic, engaging St Preux in lovers' banter and even showing jealousy when he seems too attentive to a woman at a social gathering. She shows her practical side, engaging, when her parents are away, a thatch-roofed milkmaids' hut as a place for meetings with St Preux--the milkmaids, she tells him, "know enough to keep for others the secret which they need kept for themselves." Her compromised position no longer seems to trouble her. "How dearly am I loved," she exults, "and how delighted I am to be so! Father, mother, friend, lover--I cannot cherish all who surround me enough...It seems that all the sweetest sentiments in the world continually seek out my soul." Over-confident, she cunningly arranges for St Preux to spend the night in her Clarens bedroom.

*   *   *

Of course the lovers are discovered and melancholy events follow. But here I shut the book and made my way to the dock at Vevey for the short boat trip to Clarens.

Even Shelley had been disappointed when he got to Clarens. "I never felt more strongly than on landing at Clarens, that the spirit of old times had deserted its once cherished habitation," he wrote to Peacock. Today Clarens is a sprawl of Edwardian villas and modern apartment blocks spreading along the lake and up the hillside behind. It was raining hard when we left Vevey and the cloud was still thick when we arrived at the Clarens landing stage, the humid dullness of the atmosphere enough to depress the spirits of the most ardent pilgrim. A group of pensioners were on the boat. I sometimes wonder, when in London, where all the old people have gone (people of my age, that is). Now I know. They are traveling to places like this. As they scattered along the lake, I feel sure, they were not sharing Shelley's illusion that "Julia [sic] and St Preux walked on this terraced road looking towards these mountains which I now behold; nay, treading on the ground where I now tread."

From the little harbor I walked straight up the hill past 1960's concrete and glass apartment buildings. I crossed the line of the railway. At the top, amidst suburban developments ("Les Crettes"), but with a few fields of vines here and there, there is an "Ave des Bosquets de Julie." Even in 1816 it was an attraction; Shelley was directed to the "bosquet de Julie" by the landlady of the lodging where he stayed. Then it was more rural. "It is indeed Julia's wood," Shelley persuaded himself. "The hay was making under the trees; the trees themselves were aged, but vigorous, and interspersed with younger ones, which are destined to be their successors, and in future years, when we are dead, to afford a shade to future worshippers of nature, who love the memory of that tenderness and peace of which this was the imaginary abode." Shelley walked with Byron through vineyards "whose narrow terraces overlook this affecting scene," and Shelley felt compelled to repress "tears of melancholy transport which it would have been so sweet to indulge, immeasurably, even until the darkness of night had swallowed up the objects which excited them."

Even so, Shelley found the actual site of the *bosquet*, where Julie and St Preux had exchanged their first passionate kiss, disappointing. Shelley discovered that "the precise spot was now utterly obliterated." This was the work of the monks of the convent which now owned the land, giving Shelley the opportunity to condemn the "system of prescriptive religion" which was invariably "inimical to natural sensibility."

Shelley and Byron ascended to the Chateau along a road which wound through woods of walnut and chestnut. On the terrace they gathered roses "in the feeling that they might be the posterity of some planted by Julie's hand," and scattered their dead and withered leaves "to the absent."

The trees, and their descendants, are long gone. At the summit of the hill there is a large 19th century house ("Le Chateau"), now divided into flats, with an observation tower. Around the grounds of this house circles the "Chemin de la Nouvelle Héloise", so perhaps there are still some inhabitants who are, as Shelley found, "impressed with an idea, that the persons of that romance had actual existence." Judging by the number of signs with the same message (Passage Interdit; Propriété Privée; Entrée Interdite) the people who live in the place must sometimes be bothered by fans of Julie, though on this occasion it was eerily deserted; nothing but trim gardens, clipped hedges--no hay makers or vineyard workers-- not a living soul.

The view from the top is still magnificent, though; across the lake to the massive peak of the Grammont with St Gingolph at its foot. A few wisps of cloud hung about, half way up the mountains, in the still air.

Rousseau's Julie

Returning to Vevey from Clarens I dined at the Auberge de la Clef near the market square. A marble plaque proclaims that Jean-Jacques Rousseau was there in 1730. A quotation from Rousseau's *Confessions* follows: "j'allai a Vevey...loger a la Clef...je pris pour cette ville un amour qui m'a suivi dans tous mes voyages." What the quotation omits is that Rousseau was in Vevey alone and miserable, moping and longing for Mme de Warens who had lived there and with whom he was in love. (The rocks at Meillerie actually look across the lake not to Clarens and the supposed abode of Julie, but to Vevey and the home of Mme de Warens.) As the rain battered the roof of the inn while I ate my dinner I thought about the woman who had, in part, inspired Rousseau's Julie.

Rousseau was born in 1712, in, as he often boasted, Geneva. His mother died shortly after his birth and his father went away leaving him, in effect, an orphan. At sixteen he ran away from an unhappy apprenticeship. In Catholic Savoy Rousseau met a priest who saw in the young exile from Calvinist Geneva a likely convert to the true faith. He directed him to Annecy with an introduction to a lady there who, herself a convert, took an interest in other candidates for conversion. Arriving in Annecy, what Rousseau found when he first met Francoise Louise Eleanore de la Tour, Baronne de Warens, took him by surprise. He had expected to find a middle-aged, pious lady. Instead he saw a young blonde woman of great beauty. "I saw a face steeped in charm, beautiful blue eyes full of sweetness, a dazzling complexion, and the outline of an enchanting bosom...I became hers at that moment." It was Palm Sunday, 21 March 1728; and it was to be the most important meeting of his life. (In his *Confessions* Rousseau wrote that the spot where they met should be enclosed in a railing of gold. This was actually done in 1928 on its 200th anniversary.)

Mme de Warens, though a bit buxom for some tastes, was undoubtedly a handsome woman and a captivating one. A friend described her coloring as "lily and rose" and noted the striking vivacity of her eyes. She seemed unpretentious and "everything about her breathed sincerity, humaneness and kindness." She was, however, also a schemer, improvident and extravagant, a thief and probably a kind of spy, none of which detracted from her charms. She was born in Vevey, thirteen years before Rousseau first saw the light in Geneva. Like Rousseau, her mother died in childbirth and, since she did not live with her father, she too was almost an orphan. She was brought up by aunts and, after the death of her father, by legal guardians. She married at fourteen. After a short time in Lausanne the couple moved to Vevey and their handsome house is still there, not far from the Auberge de la Clef. She had no children and, perhaps as a way of keeping herself occupied, embarked on what was to be the first of her many disastrous financial ventures, a stocking factory. After a while, she decided to jettison responsibility for the factory and her husband as well. Pleading ill health, she crossed the lake to Evian for a cure. Without telling her husband she took with her the family silver, her linens and her jewelry. At Evian she ostentatiously declared her conversion to Catholicism and threw herself under the protection of Victor Amadeus, the king of Sardinia, who was ruler of Savoy. She fled to Annecy accompanied by an armed guard provided by the king. She was then twenty-seven.

Mme de Warens received some support from the Church for her help in converting Protestants, and from the King for some sort of covert intelligence work of a nature not precisely known, but her financial situation was always precarious. She was a gambler by instinct, investing in risky ventures that invariably ended badly. When Rousseau met her she had a business concocting herbal medicines. She was also extravagant, maintaining at Annecy an extensive household with several servants in a handsome house with a view of fields and orchards. Rousseau soon settled in comfortably. Also in the household was Claude Anet, Mme de Warens' assistant in the herbal medicine business, who was also her lover, though Rousseau seems to have been unaware of that.

Rousseau's relationship with Mme de Warens was equivocal. While he was devoted to her, and the attraction was clearly erotic, she was a kind of mother figure for him. He referred to her as "Maman" and she called him her "petit". He would kiss and caress her, was jealous if he thought she was too attentive to another, and was driven to fetishistic raptures by her possessions--even kissing furniture which she had touched. There was something playful in the relationship too; they would chase one another around the house, laughing; and, when making preserves, she would let him lick the sticky syrop from her fingers.

In spite of this, amused and flattered by his attention as she probably was, Mme de Warens made efforts to get Rousseau out of the house and into a vocation, at first as a priest, then as a musician. Also, she needed to go away on one of her mysterious intelligence missions. So Rousseau left Annecy and became a wanderer for over a year, going to Lausanne, Paris, Lyon and elsewhere. It was during the course of these travels that he stopped at the Auberge de la Clef at Vevey, lonely and sad and missing "Maman." When he learned that Maman wanted him back he left at once to join her at Chambery where she was then living.

Reunited with Maman Rousseau found that his previous infatuation had somewhat abated. Desperate longing had given way to a quieter and more secure kind of love. He remained at Chambery for ten years. Though Mme de Warens tried repeatedly to find regular employment for him none of these efforts worked out. Rousseau became a part time music teacher

Mme de Warens had a garden outside Chambery and it was there one day that she coolly proposed that they become lovers. When it finally happened Rousseau's response was mixed. "For the first time I saw myself in the arms of a woman, and a woman I adored", he later wrote. "Was I happy?" he asked himself. "No, I tasted pleasure, but I know not what invincible sadness poisoned its charm. I felt as if I had committed incest." Rousseau, for all his love for her, could not see Mme de Warens as a fully sexual woman. With her, he wrote, his pleasure was "always disturbed by a feeling of sadness, by a secret clenching of the heart that I could overcome only with difficulty, and instead of congratulating myself on possessing her, I reproached myself for defiling her." To warm up his desire he fantasized about other women while he was in bed with Mme de Warens. While she was no longer exactly his old "Maman", she fell short of being the ideal lover of his imaginings.

The most satisfying phase of the affair took place after Claude Anet died and the medicine business failed. Mme de Warens rented the farm at Les Charmettes in the hills just outside Chambery. This pleasant house, which still exists, became for Rousseau a place of love and tranquility, remembered by Rousseau in later life in a kind of golden haze. Some of this happiness, for Rousseau, seems to have been due not only to the rural setting but also to the newly chaste nature of his relations with his mistress. They had separate bedrooms and when, after his morning walk, he would greet her, still in her bed, it was with an embrace "as pure as it was tender, its very innocence giving it a charm that is never joined to sensual pleasure." This was not enough for "Maman". She needed a competent farm manager (Rousseau could never be that) and something more from a man-about-the-house. In 1737 she hired a young man, the son of the keeper of the castle of Chillon, who soon took on the twin duties of farm manager and lover. (Like Anet before him he became her partner in her next, and equally disastrous, financial scheme; this time it was coal and copper mines.) In 1739 Mme de Warens was able to find a post for Rousseau as tutor for a family in Lyon and after ten years Rousseau's life with Mme de Warens ended.

Lyon, Venice, Paris--and fame at last for Rousseau; by which time he had settled down with Therese Levasseur, a semi-literate laundress he had met in Paris. She became his mistress as well as his servant and companion, eventually even his wife. Although Rousseau said he never loved her, they lived contentedly together. As well as her rapacious family, Therese brought to Rousseau five children each of whom was, shockingly, deposited at birth with the foundling hospital. This shameful fact, which neither Rousseau nor his biographers have succeeded in explaining away, was a stain on Rousseau's character which was often cited by his enemies--and he had many enemies--particularly since it was in such egregious conflict with his theories.

Mme de Warens wrote to Rousseau years after he had left Les Charmettes to ask him for money. All her speculations having failed, she was desperate. Rousseau dismissed her appeal with a meagre contribution. In 1754 Rousseau took Therese with him to visit her. It was their last meeting and it was a painful one. "I saw her again," he wrote, "in what a state, my God! What degradation! What remained of her original virtues? Was this the same Mme de Warens, once so brilliant...? How it broke my heart." During the eight more years she had to live, Mme de Warens sank deeper into hopeless poverty and illness. She died abandoned by all, every financial project collapsed, her belongings seized and auctioned off to meet the demands of her creditors.

*   *   *

If the first woman to have influenced the creation of Julie was the object of a youthful crush the second ignited a middle-aged infatuation.

71

In the spring of 1756 Rousseau left Paris for reasons both practical and philosophical Though he said he was fleeing the distractions and corrupt society of the city there was nothing too rustic about the house he was retreating to. The Hermitage was a comfortable house with a large garden, made available to Rousseau and his household (Therese and her mother) by one of Rousseau's admirers, Mme d'Epinay. It was a former hunting lodge in the grounds of her chateau of La Chevrette, north of Paris in the valley of Montmorency. The house had been handsomely restored by Mme d'Epinay for Rousseau's use. For that purpose she had diverted men and materials from the extensive works being carried out at the chateau by her husband, who had made a fortune as a tax farmer.

The setting for the novel was already in Rousseau's mind. Apart from his memory of his visit to Vevey in 1730, Rousseau had been taken on the lake when he visited Switzerland in 1754. In his *Confessions* he described a boat trip similar to that taken by Shelley and Byron in 1816. "We spent seven days," he wrote, "making the circuit in the finest possible weather." (In that respect at least it was unlike the 1816 expedition.) "I retained the clearest memories of these spots at the other end of the lake [Rousseau meant at the opposite end to Geneva]...which I described some years afterwards in *La Nouvelle Heloise."*

Rousseau had already started planning the novel when one day, sitting alone in the garden at the Hermitage, he was overcome with sadness at the thought that he might never have a passionate love. "How could it be," he lamented, "that with such inflammable feelings, with a heart entirely moulded for love, I had not at least once burned with love for a definite object? Devoured by a need to love that I had never been able to satisfy I saw myself coming to the gates of old age, and dying without having lived." It seems that what Rousseau was missing was something different from what he had enjoyed with Mme de Warens, that is, real erotic passion. Meditating on this theme in the garden Rousseau started thinking about all the women he had loved, and soon found himself surrounded by a mental seraglio of houris--Mme de Warens conspicuously not among them. Unless, that is, she was present as a *genius loci* in the landscape Rousseau chose for his story--the lake "around which my heart has never ceased to wander", where the "richness and variety of the landscape, the magnificence and majesty of the whole, which charms the senses, moves the heart and elevates the soul."

Soon appeared a woman like those he had dreamed of. Elizabeth Sophie Francoise, Comtesse d'Houdetot was a cousin of Mme d'Epinay and the mistress of Rousseau's friend Jean-Francois de St Lambert. She was twenty-six and the mother of three children. It seems likely she had never loved her husband, but he was a friend of St Lambert and entirely approved of the arrangement. She was not particularly pretty, and marked by smallpox, but she had naturally thick black hair. Above all, she was good humored, a bit scatter-brained perhaps, and had great sweetness of nature and an unaffected combination of gaucheness and grace which was very appealing. It is not hard to see why anyone would fall in love with her.

The first visit Mme d'Houdetot made to the Hermitage was memorable. Her carriage got stuck in the mud and she decided to go the rest of the way on foot, struggling through the mire. She arrived filthy and in a pair of borrowed boots, her shoes having been lost in the mud--and laughing. Therese loaned her some clean clothes and she stayed for a meal. "Our meeting was so gay", Rousseau wrote, "she was quite delighted and seemed inclined to come again."

That was in the autumn of 1756. She did not come back until the following spring. By then Rousseau was hard at work on the novel, having already written "several letters that betray the ecstatic state in which I wrote them." Mme d'Houdetot's second visit was as memorable as the first. She arrived alone, on horseback and in man's clothes. Rousseau was charmed and "this time," he confides, "it was love...the first and only love in all my life." Rousseau passed from a state where he was "intoxicated with love that lacked an

73

object" to transferring to Mme d'Houdetot (or Sophie as he soon started calling her) all the attributes with which he had already invested his fictional Julie. Sophie he soon saw as an idealized version of herself, "endowed with all the perfection with which I... had embellished the ideal of my heart." This took some stretch of the imagination on Rousseau's part. He gave Julie, in his instructions to the novel's illustrator, the blonde hair and fair complexion of Mme de Warens; but in Rousseau's mind virtue and innocence went with fair hair--dark-haired girls could be clever or even naughty. More relevantly, the gayety, high spirits and freedom of behavior of Sophie, her undoubted femininity mingled with a seductive tom-boyishness--makes her superficially a very different, and one might say more attractive, person than the innocently virtuous Julie; innocent, that is, until we remember that it is Julie who takes control of the sexual encounters with St Preux.

Rousseau and Sophie started taking long walks in the forest. Intimacy progressed. She allowed him to caress her and engage in amorous conversation. He spent days with her and, on one famous occasion, on a grass bank beneath a blossoming acacia, Rousseau found words to express "all that is lovable and pleasing in the feelings that the most tender and ardent passion can breathe into a man's heart", drawing tears from Sophie. He kissed her. "What a kiss! But that was all."

Sophie always maintained that she allowed Rousseau to go no further and that she was faithful to St Lambert, though she allowed Rousseau to spend a night in her bedroom. As she said "my heart cannot love twice." What could she have seen in Rousseau, an aging, penniless, misanthrope, to compete with St Lambert, a dashing poet and soldier, handsome and charming, and a notoriously successful seducer? Of course, Rousseau had the glamour of literary celebrity and Sophie clearly enjoyed the attention. Since Sophie was still alive when Rousseau published his *Confessions*, he had reason to be discrete; but I imagine what she said was true, although she allowed Rousseau to go quite far in his attentions. In a letter to her--which he did not send--Rousseau wrote, towards the end of the affair, "Oh Sophie, I implore you, do not be embarrassed about the friend you sought...Am I not yours? Did you not take possession of me?..." He adds, suggestively, "I shall not remind you of what happened in your park or in your bedroom..." and refers to his " burning lips" which "would never again lay my soul on your heart with my kisses" as well as "that heavenly tremor" and, "that inexpressible moment." All this may just be exaggeration for effect, but the words "when my mouth dared to press against yours, sometimes at least I felt a response" may well have been accurate.

While ardent, Rousseau also took a perverse pleasure in self-denial. Perhaps it would be fairer to say that, for Rousseau, the effects of passion on the active imagination were more interesting than the satisfaction of sexual desire, however pressing. It may be significant that in the detailed instructions which Rousseau gave to the artist Gravelot for illustrations to the novel the depiction of the famous kiss exchanged by Julie and St Preux under the arbor ("Le Premier Baiser de l'Amour") was to show not the kiss itself but its effect on the actors—Julie swooning into the arms of Claire.

However that may be, and whatever may have happened in Sophie's bedroom, the strongest impression given by Rousseau is one of almost unendurable frustration--relieved sometimes by orgasm, if not in Sophie's arms then on his own. Walking to meet her he would sometimes, as he admits in his *Confessions*, pause on the way to masturbate, arriving "weak, exhausted, worn out and scarcely able to stand up." He invested this frustration in his character St Preux, the mournful outsider who lives for love, but who gets love returned to him in the end.

After a month of this Sophie began to worry about what St Lambert's reaction would be when he returned from his military posting abroad. Although he was a good friend to Rousseau, this was all going a bit too far. A complicating factor was the jealousy of Mme d'Epinay. She was being kept informed of the affair by

Therese, who must have been jealous herself. The outcome was that Sophie avoided meeting Rousseau, writing to say she hoped they would remain friends; and Rousseau--as usual seeing conspiracies and enemies everywhere--quarreled bitterly with Mme d'Epinay which caused him to leave the Hermitage. The only one of the group whose behavior was irreproachable was St Lambert, who remained on friendly terms with Rousseau; but, with his equable temperament, he had a gift for friendship--he remained always on good terms with Sophie's estranged husband.

Sophie and St Lambert remained together until he died, at the age of eighty-seven, in 1803. When she was eighty Sophie made light of the episode saying of Rousseau that he "was alarmingly ugly and love did not make him any more attractive, but he was touching. I treated him with gentleness and kindness; he was an interesting madman." She died in 1813. A few years before her death she visited Rousseau's tomb and wept. For whom? For the "interesting madman" or for Sophie as she was then?

* * *

With the end of the affair with Sophie and his removal from the Hermitage Rousseau recommenced work on his novel. Now, though, from a sadder perspective, as if acknowledging to himself that romantic love has to be outgrown and that his obsessive passion could be transformed into something healthier.

Rousseau picked up the story at the point when Julie's father discovers her affair with St Preux. Julie's mother collapses and then dies. Her father, in a rage, beats Julie mercilessly. This causes her to miscarry the baby conceived from St Preux. Julie falls ill. Warned that Julie is in peril of her life unless he gives her up, St Preux leaves on a long sea voyage.

Julie's illness, nearly fatal, was smallpox, which disfigured her, but clearly more severely than Sophie's scars, since Julie writes to her cousin: "They exist no longer, those beauties of my face..." Although an English friend of St Preux, Lord Bomston (why do the French of that period always give English characters such ridiculous names?) offers to give him an estate to make him eligible to marry Julie, Julie's father will have none of it. He insists on her marriage to his friend, Monsieur de Wolmar. Julie dismisses St Preux with words similar to those employed by Sophie in dismissing Rousseau: "If you are losing a tender mistress you are gaining a faithful friend."

Wolmar, as Julie describes him, is no romantic hero--elderly (like Rousseau, almost fifty), sensible, decorous, cool, never gay or sad but always content. Julie is unable to find "passion of any kind in him except that which he has for me." And this passion is "so even and so temperate that one would say that he loves only so much as he wishes to and that he wishes to only as much as reason permits." Julie explains to St Preux her new perspective: "What has long misled me and what perhaps still misleads you is the thought that love is necessary to form a happy marriage...Love is accompanied by a continual uneasiness over jealousy or privation, little suited to marriage, which is a state of enjoyment and peace."

Fortified by these insights, Julie settles down to a seemingly contented marriage, becoming a matron and mother and helping with the management of the estate at Clarens. But Julie is still troubled by memories of St Preux, "memories as fearful as the original sensation." "I am tender in reminiscing. I am ashamed to feel myself crying," she confesses; "I cannot forget that unfortunate man." She tells herself that her tears are no more than tears of pity, of regret, of repentance even. "Love has no more share in them. Love is nothing to me now..."

After four years' absence St Preux returns. Wolmar, to whom Julie has told everything, invites St Preux to live with them and be a tutor to their children. Despite the smallpox, St Preux finds Julie even more attractive than before; having put on weight only added to her beauty and she has a freer air and franker manners in place of her former girlish timidity. They have changed, but St Preux loves her still.

As a symbolic demonstration to St Preux of the governance Julie exercises over her emotions, she shows him her private garden. Here are combined order and control on rational principles, together with a romantic taste for wild and uncultivated nature--a taste which can only be satisfied by the employment of artifice, as Julie explains. Nature has done everything, she says, "but under my direction, and there is nothing here which I have not ordered." Rousseau thus throws his influence behind the changing taste in garden design, associated mainly with England and the influence of writers such as Pope and Horace Walpole.

Wolmar has clearly had a strong influence on Julie. He is portrayed as a rather bloodless rationalist. "I am one of those men," he states, "whom people think they are truly insulting when they call them insensible, that is, when they say they have no passion which diverts them from following the true direction of mankind. Little susceptible of pleasure and of grief, I even experience only very faintly that sentiment of self interest and of humanitarianism which makes the affections of others our own...My only active principle is a natural love of order..If I have any ruling passion it is that of observation. I like to read the hearts of men." In this vein of experiment Wolmar takes St Preux to the grove where he first made love to Julie and declares to him and to Julie that the three of them will be united in a lasting attachment. As a test of this, Wolmar leaves them both together and goes away for a week.

A few days after Wolmar's departure Julie and St Preux take a boat on the lake. Caught in a storm (at the very place, Byron remarked to Shelley, that they were almost shipwrecked), St Preux steered the boat to Meillerie. The storm threatened to drive the boat onto the rocks, but they make it ashore in safety. After a meagre meal, St Preux takes Julie to the isolated spot where he had once spent a miserable and lonely exile. On the height, amidst the forest trees and the streams fed by melting snow, St Preux shows Julie the rock where he had carved her name so long ago along with verses from Petrarch and Tasso. He recalls to Julie his tormenting love and the anguish with which, from this spot, he had gazed longingly at her house across the lake. As St Preux approached the cliff Julie grasps his hand. "Let us go, my friend. The air of this place is not good for me," she says.

St Preux and Julie return to the boat and in the moonlight, and in silence, recross the lake. Half way across, St Preux is seized by a violent temptation to throw Julie and himself into the water to drown together. But he "wept hard and long and was comforted." "Our hearts have never ceased to hear each other," he says. Julie agrees but in a changed voice says that this must be the last time they will "speak in this manner."

Rousseau now inserts into the novel a long digression describing the manner by which Wolmar, with the assistance of Julie, manages his estate. His methods are cold, rational, manipulative (as far as his workers are concerned), scientific, effective and authoritarian. There is much in this description of an enlightened dictator in his little realm, run on the approved principles of the *philosophes*, that reminds us of Thomas Jefferson's aspirations for his Monticello estate.

Leaving aside the details of Wolmar's estate management, and skipping over the various sub-plots concerning Julie's cousin Claire and St Preux's friend Lord Bomston, we move to the conclusion of Rousseau's story. St Preux and Julie are resigned to a loving friendship--"after having been what we were, to be what we are today--that is a real triumph of virtue. The reason for ceasing to love can be a vicious one; that which changes a tender love into a friendship no less vigorous could not be equivocal." Julie, in a final episode, goes to the castle at Chillon, accompanied only by her children. There one of the children falls into the lake while walking along the path at its edge. Julie jumps in to save him. As a result she catches a fatal fever.

On her deathbed Julie writes to Wolmar telling him that she is content to "die as I have lived, worthy of being your wife..I shall tell you nothing more." She adds that Wolmar was "of all men the one who was best for me, the only, perhaps, with whom I could establish a good household and become a deserving woman!" This cool farewell seems to the reader to be as much as the frigid Wolmar deserves. She gives a letter to Wolmar addressed to St Preux which is couched in more emotional terms.

In her final letter to St Preux Julie confesses that she has deluded herself when she thought she was cured of her love for him. She is thankful for the delusion but now, nearing death, she acknowledges what is in her heart. "Everything which was dependent upon my will was devoted to my duty. If my heart, which was not dependent on it, was devoted to you, that was my torment and not my crime. I have done what I ought to have done; my virtue remains unblemished, and my love has remained without remorse." At last, "the virtue which separated us on earth will unite us in the eternal dwelling. I am dying in this sweet hope, only too happy to purchase at the price of my life the right of loving you forever without crime and of telling you so one more time."

*   *   *

It is more than likely that Shelley only read the first part of the novel when he was on the lake with Byron. It was the ecstasies of the protagonists' passion which seemed to inspire him, not Rousseau's views on duty and renunciation. Still, the second part of the novel, jarring and digressive as it often is, forces certain insistent questions. We can accept that passionate love does not last, ardor decays into habit, and the patriarchal domain ruled over by Wolmar is in many ways idyllic--but can we say that Julie was happy even though she still loved St Preux? Passion is a torment, but devotion to duty, however satisfying, can be arid. Rousseau had to kill Julie to get this admission, but is there not something pathetic, and sad, in her hope for a place for her love for St Preux in the hereafter?

Does Rousseau not admit that he has failed to solve the problem of happiness?

Rousseau would probably say that this is the wrong question. Because he was aware of the power of feeling it could not be surrendered to without resistance; and Wolmar, for all his coolness, makes a better husband than St Preux ever would have. Passion, at the end, subsides but love remains without its former urgency. The final note is not renunciation but resignation; that is the way life has to be. Julie dies, as we all must, but at her death reveals that she has let nothing go but her life. If it is happiness in this life we are after, then that is something we can only find within ourselves.

Rousseau had written in *Emile* that "a truly happy being is a solitary being." Towards the end of his life, in the book called *Reveries of the Solitary Walker*, Rousseau came fully to accept that this was the only happiness attainable. In his Fifth Walk he describes the state which he says he often experienced on the Island of St Pierre or drifting in a boat on the lake, where his soul found a resting-place "secure enough to establish itself and concentrate its entire being there," with no past or future thoughts but where time is nothing in an indefinite present, and with no feeling other than the "simple feeling of existence, a feeling that fills our soul entirely." As long as this, almost mystical, state lasts "we can call ourselves happy, not with a poor, incomplete and relative happiness such as we find in the pleasures of life, but with a sufficient, complete and perfect happiness which leaves no emptiness to be filled in the soul."

A central preoccupation of Rousseau was always the tension between solitude and society. An orphan, a youthful wanderer, a solitary thinker never comfortable in the salons of Paris, he made solitary man the starting point of his speculations. This putative natural man, which he postulated in his Second Discourse (*On the Origin of Inequality*), has been well described as an affectless hominid lacking everything that makes us human. The picture has no historical or anthropological validity; even as an hypothesis it makes no sense.

We are each born into a community of some sort. Moreover, there is no thought without language and language is, of necessity, a communal enterprise. But Rousseau used this notional creature as an intellectual construct providing a point from which to see ourselves more clearly as we now are. The point of view might be that of a new-born child, all ego with none of that consciousness of the opinion of others which throws us outside ourselves--what Rousseau calls *amour propre*--unburdened by the need to compete, to play a role, to excel, to conform. From this point of departure we can endeavor to so live as to be more truly ourselves, to separate needs from wants, to acknowledge our authentic nature--in effect, to be happy.

And yet, in the reflections during his Tenth Walk, the last of his *Reveries*, left unfinished at his death and written exactly fifty years after he first met Mme de Warens, it was his time with her at Les Charmettes that he remembered as being "that one short time in my life when I was myself, completely myself, unmixed and unimpeded, and when I can genuinely claim to have lived." At the farm, and surrounded by the loving presence of a "gentle and indulgent woman" he succeeded in imparting to his "still simple and naive soul the form which best suited it and which it has retained ever since." His taste for solitude and contemplation grew up in his heart "along with the expansive and tender feelings which are best able to nourish it." He was, as he says, "perfectly free or better than free" because he was "subject only to my own affections and did only what I wanted to do."

We have all had experiences of this kind, moments when we have escaped constraint into an unaffected state of emotional freedom, where we are simply ourselves. These are the experiences of late childhood, which are encountered not in complete solitude but in a protected environment such as Rousseau found at Les Charmettes and which most fortunate children at some time enjoy. I can remember many instances of this in my own life, an early one being at my first boarding school when I was about ten years old. I wandered into the school kitchens one morning. I should have been in class, but the cooks accepted my presence without comment and continued their quiet banter. The place was warm and smelled delicious. The cooks chaffed me in a friendly way as I helped them with their tasks. I was there all day. That evening my form master asked me where I had been, why I had missed all my lessons. When I told him I had been in the kitchen with the cooks his normally sharp features relaxed into an expression I could not interpret, but was certainly not one of reproof, and he turned away without a word.

VIII

Vevey -- Grand Hotel

When my steamer first crossed the lake on the way to Vevey the water was glassy smooth. A mist hung low on the mountains. By the time we reached the middle of the lake the air became thick with a milky vapor. About mid day dark clouds rolled in and it rained intermittently, but the water was still smooth when not pricked by the downpour. Beneath the clouds the western horizon gleamed strangely over the darkening water.

When we reached Vevey the steamer docked at the market square in the centre of town. Superficially, the town had not changed much from what I remembered many years before. Shelley described it in 1816 as "a town more beautiful in its simplicity than any I have ever seen," and its market place still "looks directly upon the mountains of Savoy and La Valais, the lake, and the valley of the Rhone."

But, as I stepped ashore, there was a mighty growl of thunder. It seemed to be saying to me "Don't go back; don't ever go back." I felt as if an inevitable and bitter disappointment was lying in wait for me. If Vevey appeared the same, after sixty years, to my first glance, it was profoundly different. The 18th and 19th century houses in the town had been restored and maintained, but most of the shops were full of the kind of expensive goods one could not imagine anyone actually buying. Standing at the edge of the market square, my back to the rain-spattered lake, I wondered why I had come to this place. If I had expected it to be the same, I should have been aware that I had myself changed so much that even if the town had been frozen in time I could not see it with the eyes of my much younger self. Exactly half a century before the year I was standing there my father had died; my mother had died just thirty years later. My sister had died seven years ago that very summer. Even if the place had stayed the same and I had been able to encounter my boyhood self there, still, there was no one to verify that impression or greet that ghost.

I took a room over a restaurant in the market square.

*   *   *

That night I slept fitfully. My family again entered my thoughts, particularly my mother, whom I imagined sitting on the terrace of the Grand Hotel de Vevey. It was hardly surprising she should have been present. No mother and son have been closer than we were in those years. We had the same tastes and interests, laughed at the same jokes, mocked the same absurdities. The things we did together, the places we went--the theatre, antique shops and art galleries, country houses--were responded to in a mutuality of discovery and delight. I have sometimes wondered about my mother's relationship with her own parents. Did she share any of this texture of experience with them? I know she worshiped her father and her childhood reminiscences mainly featured him in his roles as cowboy, doctor, politician,-- hero in fact. But would she have shared with him her love of literature and art? Her father died when I was a baby; her mother died before I was born. Though my mother spoke seldom of her mother she left me a few hints, along with the gentle, almost wistful, face which I see in my grandmother's photograph.

My grandmother's family were Irish Presbyterians but left Ireland long before the separation of Ulster from the rest of Ireland. While Irish, they were neither members of the Anglican Ascendancy nor part of the mass of landless Catholics; they were neither of the Establishment nor the illiterate poor. They were the main class of emigrants from Ireland to America before the great famine in the Nineteenth Century. They often came with some capital and a tradition of industry and thrift. The grandfather of the novelist Henry James, who made a fortune in America, was one of these. My grandmother's father was a successful banker. If my grandmother's Irishness was attenuated after generations in America it was strong, though it might appear frail, like the fine Belleek porcelain my mother inherited from her.

I was reminded that my mother claimed some of this Irishness, though in her it was overlaid by Americanness and Anglophilia, when I came across several books bearing her Wellesley College bookplate. They were romantic novels by a now deservedly forgotten author, Donn Byrne, and I remember my mother once telling me she could not get enough of them when she was about twenty years old, a time of life when over-written romances have a strong attraction. Byrne, an Ulster Protestant and fervently Irish, seems to have been as romantic a figure as anything in his fictions. He died at forty when his car plunged over a cliff near his house, Coolmain Castle, in County Cork. Holding these books I caught, like the sound of a faint melody, the memory of Ireland bequeathed to my mother.

*   *   *

A directory of hotels in Vevey in 1900 shows the Grand at the top of the list, with two hundred rooms and a "parc de 50,000 metres." The directory listed its other attractions, some of which I recalled to memory, such as the "port et embarquement spéciaux pour yachts et bateaux a vapeur; bains du lac; deux lawn-tennis," and the "restaurant vitré" with "cuisine francaise." I had no recollection of certain other boasted features--"hydrothérapie, gymnastique... concerts tous les jours"--which may not have survived into the 1940's.

I set out in the morning along the lake shore towards the Grand Hotel, as I remembered the direction. I soon came to a small park, but this was not the park of the hotel as I remembered it. In my mind's eye I saw the view from the hotel's terrace (past the attendant chairs in which, after luncheon, a few guests might be slumped) and the sweep of the park down to the lake. Paths took meandering routes between banks of dense laurels. (There were places there where hours could be spent with a book undisturbed.) Between the trunks of great trees the lake shone with a vital tone of blue. But nothing now remained of this remembered "parc de 50,000 metres". However, in a short while, I came upon the little yacht harbor with its stone walls which I remembered (port et embarquement spéciaux pour...etc). But the hotel which once rose in its great park was no more, swept away to clear the site for the steel and glass modernist buildings housing the headquarters of the Nestle company. All that remains is the little harbor and some of the larger trees.

Standing by the harbor, now empty of the boats it used to shelter, and looking at the gleaming corporate edifice where the park used to be, I saw myself at age twelve running on the paths which wound through the laurels--faster! faster! At the foot of the harbor jetty was the place where the little yacht was always moored, the yacht which once made me dream of solitary voyages. I imagined I felt the cold water after the hot sun as I swam with my sister out into the lake. I remembered the sun shining through the windows onto the white table cloths in the dining room, the murmur of the waiters at the door. I also remember sometimes being bored. Apart from swimming and boating there was little for my sister and me to do and I do not remember encountering any other children at the hotel in the summers we passed there; but since we were accustomed to being on our own during the holidays neither my sister nor I saw this as in any way unusual.

Looking out on the lake, the water now placid after the rain, the lake enclosed by the distant mountains, it seemed to hold other images from the past. Above all, one episode came back to me. It must have been during our second or third summer at the hotel. My uncle Edmund from Oklahoma, the dear Uncle Ed who had been a kind of substitute father to my sister and myself during the years of the war, was with us. It must have been his first visit to Europe and the first time we had been together for several years. We rowed out into the lake in a small boat, I with my mother and sister and Uncle Ed at the oars. Some way from the shore we found ourselves in the path of the steamer going to Vevey. Instead of rowing us out of the path of the advancing steamer my uncle seemed frozen, with his head tipped down slightly. My mother called to him to row, but he sat unmoving as the steamer bore down upon us. I remember the white hull of the steamer and the sparkling drops of water cast by the churning paddle wheels. In a moment my mother and I took the oars from my uncle's hands and rowed the boat out of the steamer's path. Nothing was said as we returned to the dock. Many years later, after my uncle died, my mother recalled the incident and said she thought he had suffered a minor stroke. He might have been simply paralyzed by fear. But, whatever the cause, I remember my own feelings at the time. Uncle Ed had always been, for me, familiar and at the same time heroic, a great figure in my boyhood pantheon. And then, in an instant, I saw him a helpless old man and my world changed.

*   *   *

It is perhaps appropriate that the Grand Hotel should have been torn down to make way for a hive of modern commerce. That sort of hotel catered for a mode of tourism at the end of the 19th century which does not really exist now. The giant hotels built along the lake near Montreux, mansarded and turreted structures with balconies facing the lake, have now been turned into flats.

The glory days of Swiss tourism began after the defeat of Napoleon when swarms of British tourists came onto the continent from which they had been for so long excluded. Switzerland now rivaled Italy as the favored destination; its dramatic mountain scenery appealed to the awakened taste for wild and rugged landscapes. What had once been thought horrid and terrifying was now seen as sublime. Byron complained of the number and ignorance of English tourists, as well as the rapacity of the Swiss hoteliers who exploited them. A "parcel of staring boobies," he called these tourists, "who go about gaping and wishing to be at once cheap and magnificent." Near Chillon he encountered an English party in a carriage, a lady in it fast asleep; "fast asleep in the most anti-narcotic spot in the world--excellent!" If fatigue and boredom occasionally overcame tourists everywhere, it was the inability to respond adequately to the scenes before them which most annoyed Byron. At Chamonix, "in the very eyes of Mt Blanc," he reported, an English female tourist exclaimed to her party: "did you ever see anything more rural?--as if it was Highgate, or Hampstead, or Brompton, or Hayes--'Rural' quotha!--Rocks, pines, torrents, Glaciers, Clouds and Summits of eternal snow far above them--and 'Rural'!" The poor tourist, who, Byron admits, was "a very good kind of a woman," had not found the words ("sublime", "picturesque," perhaps?) required to express the new sensibility.

The tourists flocking to Switzerland in Byron's day, ignorant or insensitive as they may have been, were at least intrepid. To get a closer look at the mountains they had to scramble up on foot or mule back or travel by carriage on precarious roads. Another half century would pass before the golden age of alpinism in the 1850's and 60's. In 1858 the first Thomas Cook package holiday took place and with the invention of the cog railway the mountains began to be available to the train traveler. The first rail tunnel--the Gotthard--was opened in 1881. It took ten years to build and took the lives of two hundred workers. By 1888 the train had conquered the mountains. At about that time it was discovered that high mountain air was good for the sufferers of lung diseases such as tuberculosis and sanatoria, like that described by Thomas Mann in *The Magic Mountain*, were opened.

Rail travel and the taste for mountain scenery led to a boom in the building of grand hotels in Switzerland during the Belle Epoque. Fifty were built between 1834 and 1893, when the Swiss Ecole Hotelière was founded in Lausanne to train staff to operate these establishments. By the outbreak of the First World War the number of them had more than doubled.

The 1900 directory, already mentioned, which listed the Grand-Hotel de Vevey and described its attractions, also listed two other slightly smaller hotels. The Grand Hotel du Lac had a "terrasse ombragée", which sounds inviting, also a lift and electric light ("éclairage et service compris") and an "orchestre d'élite." Despite these attractions, and it having been the setting for the novel by Anita Brookner bearing its name, I decided to have a drink not at that hotel but at the third one on the list which had even stronger literary associations. That was the Grand Hotel des Trois Couronnes which was advertised as having "grand confort" but at a "prix modérés."

The Trois Couronnes was elegant but less ostentatious than the old Grand-Hotel de Vevey. In the bar there was only a well-dressed woman, in her late 50's I would guess, nervous and thin and obviously waiting for someone. A murmur of conversation came from the dining room. Unostentatiously sumptuous as the hotel was, there was an unmistakable end-of-season melancholy, which suited my mood. But it was impossible not to imagine the hotel as Henry James described it (when? 1877?), in high summer. That June, in the garden of the hotel, which seemed to me now much smaller than I had imagined, the young American, Winterbourne, was accosted by an even younger American, the irritatingly precocious brother of Daisy Miller. Daisy is the prototype of other James heroines, young American girls; candid, free, direct and spontaneous--just the qualities that got Daisy into such a lot of trouble in the rigid society of Rome's American colony. From this hotel in Vevey Winterbourne, in what has been aptly referred to as an act of calculated impropriety, took Daisy unaccompanied to visit Chillon. Later he seeks her out in Rome. As with *Childe Harold*, the last scene is at the Coliseum. It is there that Daisy's reckless appetite for life, and the malaria mosquito, prove fatal. Winterbourne, who could never take her measure, is left to console himself with an anonymous *demi-mondaine*.

IX

Interlude -- William Beckford

At a short distance from the market square at Vevey the turreted Chateau de la Tour de Peilz stands on a promontory looking across the lake to the distant mountains of Savoy. The chateau is so called because its twin towers were originally roofed with hides. In 1785 and 1786 William Beckford, the author of *Vathek*, made his home there, with his wife Lady Margaret. The place is now a Museum of Games, appropriate perhaps for an association with Beckford, that old masquerader.

Beckford always loved Switzerland, from the time when he completed his private education there at the age of eighteen; he never went to university, or even school. His immensely wealthy father, Alderman Beckford, died when William was nine years old. He grew up under the strict control of his Calvinistic mother at Fonthill Splendens, the immense house the Alderman had built on his Wiltshire estate. Switzerland was Beckford's first escape from the maternal clutches. Later there was the Grand Tour.

Beckford soon acquired a reputation as a handsome, clever, eccentric young man, an aesthete with a taste for the exotic. Beckford was also, on gaining his majority, very rich. All these attributes gained him social advantages. He entertained spectacularly. For one three day party he, with the assistance of the artist and stage designer Louderbourg, transformed Fonthill Splendens into a place of gloomy enchantment, a "Demon Temple". As Beckford, much later, recalled, his guests ("extremely youthful and lovely to look upon") wandered hand in hand through rooms from which "monotony of every kind was banished." There, along with Loutherbourg's lighting effects and drapery, "the uniform splendour of gilded roofs was partially obscured by the vapour of wood aloes ascending in wreaths from cassolettes placed low on the silken carpets in porcelain salvers of richest japan." One can imagine the effect.

Much of this taste for rich decor found its way into Beckford's novel, which he wrote in French. (He hired a translator, anonymous so far as the title page reveals, to produce the English version.) Vathek, the Caliph, is a willful and sensuous prince, clearly a self-projection of the author. His frightful mother, the Begum, is obviously intended as a vengeful portrait of Beckford's own mother. The Caliph indulges all his luxurious tastes, described at length--including a taste for wanton cruelty--and ends up, through the intervention of a demon or genie, selling his soul to the ruler of Eblis, the Nether Regions. The tale itself, for all its luxuriant descriptions, is of little interest except to the extent it reveals Beckford's oriental researches and his anxieties over his homoerotic preferences. Most of the author's imagination and skill is devoted to picturing the incidental trappings--all golden vessels, glittering jewels, sumptuous palaces, almond-eyed houris, scimitar-bearing Negro eunuchs and the like. As a fantasy it resembles less the Gothick Novel of the time (Horace Walpole's *Castle of Otranto*, say, or Matthew Lewis's *The Monk*) so much as it looks forward to J-K Huysmans and Oscar Wilde.

Beckford's tastes and behavior began to alarm his mother and his other female relatives. Added to which there was the unhealthy attachment of his cousin by marriage, Louisa, who, along with her obsessive love for Beckford, was dying of consumption. And then there was Beckford's passion for the effeminate youth, also a relative, William Courtney, known as Kitty. As an antidote to these dangerous temptations, the Begum, as Beckford called his mother, steered her son into a marriage with her chosen bride, Lady Margaret Gordon. Beckford obeyed meekly.

Lady Margaret was unaffected, physically attractive and submitted to Beckford's whims. Although at first there was no question of love on his side, she must have seemed as good a choice as any other, and, like Byron later, marriage must have appeared both inevitable and a convenient escape from perturbations of the heart. Later, Beckford came to have real love for his wife, who bore him two children, both girls.

Not long after Beckford returned from his extended honeymoon, spent mainly in Paris, disaster struck. William Courtney's aunt was married to a political lawyer, Lord Loughborough, later Lord Chancellor, who detested Beckford. Loughborough was determined to expose the scandal, as he saw it, of Beckford's relations with young Courtney, who was now seventeen. Whether or not Beckford was caught in bed with Courtney while Beckford and his wife were visiting the Courtney seat at Powderham Castle--and it seems most unlikely that this occurred--this was the story that was put about most energetically by Loughborough. Loughborough forced Courtney to hand over the extravagantly passionate letters which Beckford had written to him years before. They were, to say the least, compromising. Lady Margaret's brother stormed down to Fonthill to rescue his sister from her monster husband; but she was steadfastly loyal and refused to be rescued. The Begum, who had long known her son to be bisexual, proposed an original stratagem: Beckford should go up to London and parade about with a gaggle of Covent Garden whores to counter the rumors. Beckford wisely rejected this suggestion. In what must have seemed to Beckford a painful twist of irony the adored child to whom Beckford had addressed his passionate love letters had, by the time the scandal burst upon him, become a vapid youth for whom Beckford felt nothing but loathing.

While there was never a serious threat of prosecution for the crime of sodomy, Beckford faced a sustained campaign of innuendo and vilification. Respectable people who had heard tales of "orgies" at Fonthill--or who resented the fact that they had never been invited to these parties--were grimly satisfied that their worst impressions were true. Sir William Hamilton, another of Beckford's numerous relations, with whom Beckford had spent time as a guest in Naples (Beckford had become a great favorite of the first Lady Hamilton, who had warned him of the social consequences of his homosexual adventures), received a letter from his nephew Charles Greville. Greville retailed the story as it must have been current in the London clubs: that Beckford had gone into William Courtney's bedroom early one morning and Courtney's tutor "heard a creeking [sic] and bustle, which raised his curiosity, and thro' the key hole he saw the operation which it seems he did not interrupt, but informed [Courtney's father] and the whole was blown up." Beckford's reputation was ruined and he remained for the rest of his life a social pariah.

It was to escape from England and the scandal that pursued him that Beckford came with Lady Margaret to the Chateau de la Tour de Peilz. It was also now that they came truly to love one another. Lady Margaret had always loved Beckford and her loyalty to him turned his former indifference into real affection. Beckford's letters from Switzerland that summer reflect the peace he found there. "Calmly resigned to my present situation," he wrote, "I cling first to my tutelary Mountains...We continue the favourites of Heaven in respect to weather, having violets and wallflowers in profusion. Flies buzzing a summer song almost every day on the Terrace and now and then a butterfly by way of regale..."

Lady Margaret was pregnant when they left England and in May their second daughter was born. Then tragedy struck. Twelve days after the birth the mother died of puerpural fever. Beckford was grief-stricken. The Swiss idyll over, he returned to Fonthill with Lady Margaret's body. Coming after scandal had ruined his social existence in England the consolation of a happy domestic life had now also been taken from him. The sense of doom, of being somehow accursed, would color the rest of his long life. A year after Lady

Margaret's death he was "calling in vain upon her who can hear me
no more, the companion of my happiest hours, once so lively and
blooming, now lying cold and ghastly in the dark vaults at Fonthill,
the loveliest and most unaffected of beings who doted on her poor
William with such excessive fondness, and pardoned with such a
sweet endearing cheerfulness his childish errors. That tutelary angel
it has pleased the Great Being to take away from me, and I am now
left almost without a friend, wandering about the world, the object
of the vilest calumnies and the most capricious persecutions."

Beckford's lonely exile took him to Portugal where he was better
received than in England and made influential friends. He took up
residence at Monserrate, near Sintra. There he enlarged the house
and created a garden in the English "natural" style, an expanse
of trees, shrub-bordered paths and steep approaches. Though the
house was altered and the garden neglected by subsequent owners,
and it was later abandoned, it had a melancholy appeal for Byron
when he visited in 1809. Childe Harold found that "giant weeds a
passage scarce allow / To halls deserted, portals gaping wide…" He
found it "the most desolate mansion in the most beautiful spot I
ever beheld." It had a mournful beauty even when I was there at
the end of the twentieth century.

Byron's pilgrimage to Monserrate was prompted by his admiration
for Beckford's *Vathek*, which he first read the year of his visit. It may
have been the eastern setting, the rich prose style or even the sexual
ambiguity in the descriptions of the Caliph's androgynous lover
which attracted him. Byron thought Beckford "the great apostle
of Paederasty." It seems only too appropriate that Caroline Lamb,
when she invaded Byron's Albany rooms dressed as a boy, scribbled
"Remember me" on the fly leaf of Byron's copy of *Vathek* which she
found lying on a table. This prompted Byron later to dash off, on
the same page, his lines

> Remember thee! Remember thee!
> Till Lethe quench life's burning stream

Remorse and shame shall cling to thee,
And haunt thee like a feverish dream!

Beckford returned to England but his period of exile had produced no relaxation of his social ostracism. He settled at Fonthill but the local gentry refused to have anything to do with him. Behind the enormous wall he had built around the park he took out his frustration in architectural fantasy. Collaborating with the architect James Wyatt, Beckford constructed a gothic folly, the Abbey, into the building and furnishing of which he poured huge sums. Fonthill Splendens was mined for stone. Eventually the Abbey was surmounted by a gothic-inspired tower some 270 feet high, influenced in style by the Portuguese monastery at Batalha. The interiors were sumptuously decorated with rich hangings and gilt, the candle-lit gloom relieved by colors thrown from stained glass windows.

Even Beckford's vast wealth was not enough to sustain these expenditures and by 1821 the sale of the Abbey and the Fonthill estate became inevitable. Beckford sold the property and moved to Bath--just in time, for the tower of the Abbey soon after collapsed with a great thunder of falling masonry. In Bath Beckford built himself another tower--this one is still standing. He lived on, still collecting and decorating, into the Victorian age. *Vathek* was reissued and became modestly popular. A new generation of readers found its orientalism attractive. Beckford struck up a friendship with the young Benjamin Disraeli, who sent him a copy of his eastern romance, *Alroy*. In 1834 they met at the opera and talked together for three hours. We do not know what they talked about, but Disraeli described him as being "very bitter and *malin*, but full of warm feelings for the worthy." Once Disraeli entered Parliament their correspondence ended. Beckford died in 1844 at the age of eighty-four.

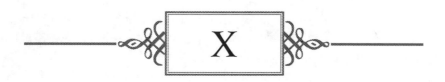

Lausanne

From Vevey Shelley and Byron sailed along the coast of the Pays de Vaud towards Lausanne. Shelley observed to Peacock that, with its villages and vineyards, the coast presented "an aspect of tranquility and peculiar beauty which well compensates for the solitude which I am accustomed to admire." The hills were crowned with woods and waterfalls echoed from the cliffs.

Though there are many more houses now, that part of the lake still retains some of that tranquility. Between the houses there are small patches of vineyard, a curious mixture of suburban and rural, and the steep hillsides above are covered with vines. Every centimeter of land appears to be tilled. There is something orderly about the land now--the houses, the road, the railway, the vines; each allotted its space without competition. Nothing is wasted, nothing extravagant, nothing out of place, no waste or uncultivated land, no large developments, nothing assertive or ugly; in fact, nothing overtly commercial. At one village near Ouchy, where poplars line the shore, two people disembark from the steamer. I am almost alone on the boat now. At the next village the hillside falls steeply to where a narrow dock protrudes into the lake. Wherever they can get a purchase the vines cover the slopes in neat rows. A crowd of children waves from the dock. A white-bearded old man smokes his pipe. Between the terraced vines enormous grey rocks break out of the soil and houses cling precariously to the hillside. It was here that Shelley observed "the traces of two rocks of immense size, which had fallen from the mountain behind." He added that one of these rocks "lodged in a room where a young woman was sleeping, without injuring her,"

The rain detained Shelley and Byron for two days in Ouchy and it was raining as my steamer proceeded to Lausanne. The waves on the lake were choppy and at mid day it was dark. The shoreline trees appeared as a bulk of indistinguishable darkness. Then the densely packed buildings of Lausanne appeared out of the mist, modern urbanism and no mistake. As the rain lessened for a time the lake changed color, reflecting the temporary brightness. The tower of Lausanne Cathedral appeared on the hill.

In Lausanne Byron insisted that Shelley accompany him to visit the house of Edward Gibbon and the decayed summer house in which he finished his great history of the Roman Empire.

Gibbon had been packed off to Switzerland by his father when, as a student at Oxford, he threatened to become a Roman Catholic. This was so alarming that the young Gibbon was put under instruction to a Calvinist minister in Lausanne. The cure was effective, in that Gibbon became a religious sceptic. Once back in England Gibbon became an MP, but he eventually returned to Lausanne where he occupied a "spacious and convenient mansion, connected on the north side with the city, and upon the south to a beautiful and boundless horizon." There he applied himself to his great work. In his Autobiography he describes his joy, mixed with sadness, on the completion of his task. "It was on the day, or rather night, of the 27th of June 1787, between the hours of eleven and twelve, that I wrote the last lines of the last page, in a summer house in my garden. After laying down my pen, I took several turns in a *berceau*, or covered walk of acacias, which commands a prospect of the country, the lake, and the mountains. The air was temperate, the sky was serene, the silver orb of the moon was reflected from the waters, and all nature was silent." His relief at being freed from his labors was soon succeeded by the melancholy thought that he had now taken leave of "an old and agreeable companion."

At the house Byron plucked some leaves from the acacia on the terrace, with its view of the lake and the mountains, in the shade of which Gibbon had walked after laying down his pen. Byron sent some of these leaves to his publisher, John Murray, in London. Shelley, rather sniffishly, refrained from gathering any acacia leaves "fearing to outrage the greater and more sacred name of Rousseau; the contemplation of whose imperishable creations had left no vacancy in my heart for mortal things." The passions of Julie and St Preux had left, for him, no room for Gibbon and Rome. "Gibbon had a cold and unimpassioned spirit." Shelley returned to the lake, now spanned by a rainbow, where the waves lashed the pier, and, his thoughts full of Julie and St Preux, gazed at some white houses across the lake which he believed to be those of Meillerie.

There is no longer any trace of Gibbon's house or the acacia terrace. In the 1780's Gibbon lived in what was then the fashionable residential part of town, called the Bourg. From its garden, Gibbon wrote, "a rich scenery of meadows and vineyards descends to the Leman Lake, and the prospect far beyond the Lake is crowned by the stupendous mountains of Savoy." Now it is the commercial centre of Lausanne and the site of Gibbon's house is occupied by a post office.

Upon Gibbon's death his extensive library was put up for sale and, in 1796, was bought through an agent by William Beckford. Beckford was in England at the time and did not view his acquisition in Lausanne until 1801. Then he shut himself up with it for six weeks, reading from morning until late at night. "The people thought me mad; I read myself nearly blind," he remembered. Beckford left the books in Lausanne and, after many years, gave them to his Swiss physician, Dr Scholl, who had also been Gibbon's doctor. The library was later dispersed.

What were Beckford's motives? He had no great interest in Roman history and detested Gibbon. On hearing of the scandal which engulfed Beckford's social life Gibbon had remarked that Beckford deserved to be shunned by polite society because, even if he were innocent of the charges against him, "some regard was due to the opinion of the world." Beckford did not let the matter rest. In his own copy of Gibbon's History he wrote a sustained piece of vituperation which, in the completeness of its hostility and glistening with such intemperate animosity, deserves to be quoted in full:

> The time is not far distant, Mr Gibbon, when your almost ludicrous self-complacency, your numerous, and sometimes apparently wilful mistakes, your frequent distortion of historical Truth to provoke a gibe, or excite a sneer at everything most sacred and venerable, your ignorance of the oriental languages, your limited and far from acutely critical knowledge of the Latin and the Greek, and in the midst of all the prurience and obscene gossip of your notes--your affected moral purity perking up every now and then from the corrupt mass like artificial roses shaken off in the dark by some Prostitute on a heap of manure, your heartless scepticism, your unclassical fondness for meretricious ornament, your tumid diction, your monotonous jingle of periods, will be still more exposed and scouted than they have been. Once fairly kicked off from your lofty, bedizened stilts, you will be reduced to your just level and true standard.

One can only guess that Beckford, in buying the books and reading his eyes out over them, was hoping to get revenge for Gibbon's insult by gathering enough material for a book or pamphlet attacking the historian. This short piece of vituperation, however, was the only result.

*   *   *

While Gibbon's house and his terrace are long since gone, his name was not entirely forgotten in Lausanne. When Charles Dickens and his family (including six children, two nurses and a dog, Timber) arrived in Lausanne in June 1846 they put up at the Hotel Gibbon. From there they moved into a rented villa on the slopes above the lake. There Dickens began to write *Dombey and Son* though he missed the long walks through the streets of London where he found his main inspiration. "I don't seem to be able to get rid of my spectres unless I can lose them in crowds," he wrote. His need to walk through streets at night was a tormenting "mental phenomenon." Clearly, the streets of provincial Lausanne could not provide what he needed. He later wrote to his friend Forster: "I was in that state in Switzerland, when my spirits sunk so, I felt myself in serious danger."

The lowering skies and the rather bleak urban landscape of Lausanne put me in a mood to feel sympathy for Dickens' plight, and some distant relation of Dickens' spectres visited me that day.

My sister had been very unhappy at her boarding school in England and it was from the complex injuries of this experience that my parents looked for a school for her in Switzerland where such institutions abounded. The school chosen was at Lausanne. It was presided over by a formidable Madame, unyielding in her strictness and snobbery. All I remember of the school itself was a spacious hall with an oversize Christmas tree, decorated with lighted candles. A maid was stationed on the staircase with a wet sponge at the end of a stick to dowse any candle that threatened a conflagration.

While my sister professed to have been reasonably happy at the school (it offered, I suppose, the full run of academic subjects though art and equestrianism seem to have been her main pursuits), is it wrong for me to date from her time there the approach, though only later becoming apparent, of certain ill-defined shades of darkness, self destructive impulses, like a shadow cast by the wings of a distant bird of prey? Thinking back on those days I now realize that there was always faintly perceptible to me then, like the vibration of a distant tremor too slight to be measurable on any normal scale, that temerity, never explicitly acknowledged, my parents felt in approaching what they must have seen as an emotional delicacy or special vulnerability in my sister. From whence, and why? It seemed impossible for me, on the Lausanne dockside, to untangle the later memories of my beloved sister from these questions-- unanswered and now unanswerable.

These sombre reflections were dispersed, however, as my steamer left Lausanne. By what seemed a miracle, the skies brightened, the sun came out and the mountains became fully visible. The slopes chequered with vineyards shed their grey cloak, the trees became distinguishable and varied shades of green could be seen along with the dark red (dried blood red) of the beech trees. The lake water lost its previous charcoal color and turned into the green of an unpolished emerald. A few sail boats bobbed on the water and a tiny flotilla of kayaks came to meet the steamer. The children stopped paddling to wave. On the Savoy shore a long roll of cloud lay like a feather boa between the lake surface and the outline of the mountains behind.

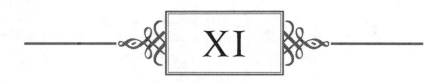

Coppet and Corinne

On Saturday the 29ᵗʰ of June 1816 Shelley and Byron left Ouchy and arrived at Montalegre, just below Cologny, on Sunday evening, ending their week's voyage around the lake. Had they wished, they might have diverted to Coppet, the chateau which Jacques Necker, the Swiss banker and adviser to the King of France, had bought in 1784 and which his daughter, Mme de Stael, had inherited on his death in 1804. Byron visited the chateau several times during that summer of 1816, but without Shelley. It was the last full summer of Mme de Stael's reign as chatelaine of Coppet. She had made it a centre of liberal resistance to Napoleon and even, as Stendhal called it, "the general headquarters of European thought."

I decided to visit Coppet; with all its associations it seemed impossible to avoid.

Byron had first met Mme de Stael in the summer of 1813, in London. She was then renowned not just for opposition to Napoleon but as an intellectual and writer. In a note to his *Bride of Abydos* Byron referred to her as "the first female writer of this, perhaps, of any age." There may have been an innuendo here which escaped her, but Mme de Stael wrote an appreciative letter--a "very pretty billet," Byron conceded. Still, in those days he found her a bit overbearing in company and excessively voluble. He wrote in his journal that she "writes octavos and *talks* folios...her works are my delight, and so is she herself, for--half an hour." If her books were delightful, in society he saw nothing but "a plain woman forcing one to listen, and look at her, with her pen behind her ear, and her mouth full of ink." By December she had won him over and he was able to record that "We are now very good friends." But, much as Byron admired her intelligence and vivacity, one cannot help thinking that her conversation might have been at times exhausting. The only person by whom she was conversationally outgunned was Coleridge. "Avec M Coleridge c'est tout a fait un monologue," she complained. At the least, her physical appearance, her personality and behavior were not of the kind that Byron would most have wished for in a woman. In February 1814 Byron wrote irritably in his journal: "More notes from Mme de Stael unanswered--and so they shall remain. I admire her ability, but really her society is overwhelming--an avalanche that buries one in glittering nonsense--all show and sophistry."

Byron's attitude to Mme de Stael had greatly changed by the time he visited Coppet in !816. He was no longer dismissive of her attentions and was grateful for the warm welcome he received, particularly congenial since Byron felt acutely his estrangement from society. For a lady as intellectually prominent as Mme de Stael, and with her erratic romantic history, Byron's scandalous reputation was unlikely to shock. Not so with all her guests. Mrs Hervey, William Beckford's sister (one would have supposed her brother's disgrace would have made the lady immune to that kind of thing) fainted at Byron's entrance and was carried out--but then came back again. "This is too much--at sixty-five years of age!" said Mme de Stael's daughter, the Duchesse de Broglie.

After he left Switzerland for Italy in October Byron wrote to Tom Moore: "I am indebted for many kind courtesies to Our Lady of Coppet--and I now love her--as much as I always did her works--of which I was and am a great admirer." By "her works" Byron meant mainly *Corinne*, the novel, published in 1807, which was the most popular thing she wrote and in which she identified closely with the heroine. In fact Germaine de Stael was often referred to, by Byron and others, as Corinne.

Mme de Stael died the summer after Byron's visits to Coppet, on July 14th. In a note to the Fourth Canto of *Childe Harold* Byron recalled with gratitude his admission to "the friendly circles of Coppet." He confessed that the loss of the mistress of Coppet would be "mourned the most where she was known the best," but, to the sorrows of her friends and dependents, he gallantly added the "disinterested regret of a stranger, who, amidst the sublime scenes of the Leman Lake, received his chief satisfaction from contemplating the engaging qualities of the incomparable Corinne."

Later visitors to Coppet, even those who had known Mme de Stael well, were impressed by the association with Byron and prepared to admit him to the circle of those close to her in life. In September 1832 Chateaubriand came with Juliette Recamier and wrote, in his usual grandiloquent style: "Golden clouds covered the horizon behind the dark line of the Jura, as if with an aureole which rose above a long coffin. I perceived on the other side of the lake Lord Byron's house, its roof touched with a ray of the setting sun..." He summoned to his memory the crowd of all those she had known, the most brilliant of the age: "It was at the foot of Mme de Stael's tomb that so many of the illustrious departed presented themselves to my memory on the same shore; they seem to come seeking the shade of their equal, so as to fly off to the heavens with her during the night, and make up her cortege."

What of the novel, *Corinne*, which Byron so admired--though, it must be said, he sometimes mocked it for its sentimentality? It was the favorite novel of his last love, Teresa Guiccioli. In 1819, when Byron and Teresa were living in Bologna, he took up her copy which, according to the biographer Iris Origo, is a "fat little volume of very small print, bound in purple plush." Byron marked some of the passages in the book and on page 92 wrote: "I knew Mme de Stael well...I little thought that one day I should think with her thoughts...she is sometimes right and often wrong, about Italy and England; but almost always true in delineating the heart." On the index page of the book Byron wrote, in English, which Teresa could not read, a declaration of his love for her: "I love you and you love me--at least you say so and act as if you did so--which last is a great consolation in all events. But I more than love you and cannot cease to love you."

*　　*　　*

Corinne, ou Italie, apart from being a hymn to the beauties and culture of Italy, is a touching love story. (The descriptions of Italian landscape and customs, and reflections on the political status of Italy, though interesting, do, for this reader at least, interrupt the main narrative unduly.) The eponymous heroine is described as resembling Domenichino's painting of the Cumaean Sibyl--a full-fleshed and dark-eyed woman in a turban. As if to emphasize that Corinne was intended to be an idealized portrait of the author, Mme de Stael favored the same headgear, as in the portrait by Gerard which hangs at Coppet. In another painting at Coppet she had herself portrayed specifically as Corinne, with lyre in hand.

In the novel, Oswald, Lord Nelvil (again, as with Lord Bomston in *Julie*, a most improbable-sounding English name) leaves his ancestral home in Scotland and travels to Italy. Melancholy, he is also brave, as he demonstrates when he rescues victims of a fire in a town. Dignified and reserved, somewhat narrow in his attitudes, he is the author's idea of the perfect type of Englishman of that time. In Rome he encounters Corinne and witnesses her coronation at the Capitol as a renowned *improvisatrice*--she declaims impromptu verses accompanying herself on the lyre or harp. Combining the talents of poet, actress and musician, she is universally acclaimed as an original genius. Oswald, at first put off by her flamboyant personality and colorful reputation, succumbs. He is attracted by her "tall, slightly plump figure" and the impression she gave of youth and happiness in a woman who is "completely natural in the ordinary relationships of life." They fall in love and travel together through Italy. Corinne instructs Oswald on the glories of Italian art and history. Oswald's reserve melts in the Italian sun and under the warmth of Corinne's love.

The passionate love of Corinne and Oswald reaches its greatest intensity in Naples. Oswald tells Corinne that this has been the happiest time of his life, but Corinne feels an ineradicable anxiety, a premonition of the doom of their love. At Posilipo they pass by torchlight through the Roman tunnel piercing the ancient Mons Pausilypus. Emerging from the tunnel Corinne tells Oswald she is taking him to the shores of Lake Averno, the mythical entrance to Hades, and the temple of the Cumaean Sibyl. There, at Cape Miseno, she takes up her lyre and declaims her improvised verses, as on the day at the Capitol in Rome when Oswald first saw her. It is a song of Italy, its glories and its tragedy. She collapses at the end. Oswald revives her. "I shall never forget this day," he says. "Could there ever be a happier one?" Corinne replies, perceptively: "I hope for no more days like this. At least, may it be blessed, as the last happy day of my life, if it is not, if it cannot be, the dawn of a lasting happiness."

The affair comes to an end when Oswald's love for Corinne is undermined by a combination of duty--the promise given by Oswald to his late father that he would marry his father's choice of bride, Lucile--and the natural attraction Oswald has to his homeland. Besides, there is the pressure of convention and the attractiveness of the innocent young Lucile, so very different from the ardent and sophisticated Corinne. Oswald decides to return to Scotland and marry Lucile. Corinne is heartbroken.

In a surprising twist Corinne reveals to Oswald that she and Lucile are half sisters. Their father had married an Italian woman, Corinne's mother, and on her death had married the mother of Lucile. Corinne had been taken to England on the death of her mother. Her father's original intention was for Corinne to marry

Oswald, but when he saw what an independent woman she had become, he preferred that Oswald marry the more conventional, and prettier, Lucile.

After a childhood spent in Italy, Corinne found England unbearable. As soon as she received her inheritance she fled back to Italy and changed her name. This allows Mme de Stael to make her feminist case as well as getting her revenge for the coolness, as she saw it, which greeted her in England as an *emigrée* escaping from the Terror. She contrasts the dismally puritanical and stultifyingly boring conditions of English life, and its repressive attitudes to women, with the open, free life of Italy where Corinne could develop her talents and where her genius would be recognized. Whether this is an accurate picture of the position of women in Italy is no matter; the case against England is made. Byron's initial reaction to what he saw as the excessive cleverness and talkativeness of Mme de Stael on his first acquaintance gives some support to her case.

Corinne and Oswald cannot live together but their love does not die. Corinne grieves in Italy. The years pass. Oswald returns to Italy with his wife and child to visit her. She is dying and refuses to see him. Oswald's feelings for Corinne become obvious to Lucile when they visit the picture gallery in Bologna and Oswald pauses before Domenichino's portrait of the Cumaean Sybil. Sensing his mind, Lucile asks him whether the Sibyl appeals to him more than Corregio's Madonna. Oswald grasps her meaning: "The Sibyl no longer utters oracles; all her genius and talent are no more--But the angelic face painted by Corregio has lost none of its charming features, and the unhappy man who caused the one so much pain will never betray the other." They return to Scotland. The last words of the novel: "Was he content with the common lot after what he had lost? I do not know, and, on that matter, I want neither to blame nor to absolve him."

*　　*　　*

There is another perspective from which to view the significance of the Domenichino portrait--apart from Mme de Stael's use of it in the novel, its slight resemblance to her, and her adoption of this mode of dress--and that is its possible associations with her father's death. Mme de Stael adored and idolized her father. Her devotion to him was extreme. Writing about *La Nouvelle Héloise* in an early appreciation she even defended Rousseau's decision to have his heroine submit to her father's orders and marry Wolmar instead of her lover St Preux. "Woe to the girl," the young author wrote, "who imagines she can resist her father!" The entreaty of a father "suspends love itself. A father who speaks like a friend, who appeals at once to nature and to the heart, is sovereign of our soul, and can obtain anything from us." Strong language from a girl who placed such a high value on independence of spirit.

When Mme de Stael returned from Germany in 1803 and found her father dead she was grief stricken. She was to mourn him for the rest of her life. It was, as she tried to explain in a reply to a letter of condolence, "not a mere father-daughter relationship: it was fraternity, love, religion, all my spiritual being." Even when they were separated, she wrote, "I believed that I was protected by him...I always called him my guardian angel...Nothing seemed beyond remedy while he lived: only since his death have I known the meaning of real terror...In his strength I found mine; my confidence depended on his support. Is he still there, my protecting genius? Will he still tell me what I should hope for or fear? Will he guide my steps?" She wrote a deeply-felt homage to him before leaving for Italy in December, 1804. There, at the Palazzo Borghese, she saw the Domenichino Sibyl, a painting "of the greatest beauty.' She noted "her hair in a turban, her red mantle." She returned to Coppet in June 1805 to begin writing *Corinne*, which was published in May, 1807.

When Corinne gives her oration in Naples Mme de Stael has her say: "The city of Cumae, the Sibyl's grotto, Apollo's temple were on this hill...The land of the Aeneid surrounds you, and the fictions sanctified by genius have become memories, of which we still seek the traces." We are reminded that the Sibyl accompanied Aeneas to the underworld where he went to seek his father Anchises, the father whose sad ghost, appearing to Aeneas, had drawn him to that place of shades. Aeneas addresses Anchises:

> tua me, genitor, tua tristis imago,
> saepius occurrens, haec limina tendere adegit

Aeneid, Book VI

If it was the father's ghost who brought Aeneas to that place, it was the Sibyl who made the journey possible. Perhaps it was this intermediary function which, consciously or not, drew Mme de Stael to the image painted by Domenichino.

Anchises shows Aeneas the future of the city and empire he will found, but what impresses us more than this in Virgil's account is the poignant greeting of the son and the long lost father in the Elysian Fields. Anyone who has lost a father must respond to it, and it seems to me unlikely that the association would have escaped Mme de Stael. Reading the passage puts me in mind of the death of my own father at the early age of fifty-six. Years after, he used to appear to me strangely in dreams. In these dreams he was not dead but living obscurely in some remote city, having taken on another life. Surprisingly, the father who appeared to me in these dreams was not my father as I knew him, and had grown to love and admire him, in the decade before his death. In these dreams he was a much younger man, reticent, elusive--an estranged ghost, or the ghost of a father I once knew but now scarcely remembered. It is as though, like Aeneas, I found a father's shade that was too elusive to be grasped, a ghost who, like Anchises, slipped through the hands of his son, weightless as wind and fugitive as a dream—"levibus ventris volucrique simillima somno."

110

XII

Detour -- Ashfold

The chateau at Coppet is a short walk from the landing stage. The chateau is painted pink with grey stone lintels to doors and windows. Most of the park has been lost to roads, the railway and houses along the lake front; but there is a fine avenue of plane trees which shade a pleasant walk. There is a sense of unpretentious comfort to the house. Although large it has an unassuming feel, fitting for a man like Necker who remained modest despite his achievements and immense wealth. At the back of the chateau its walls are within a few feet of those of the village houses as if to emphasize neighborliness and community. From the landing stage the tiled roof of the chateau rises above, yet remains a part of, the surrounding town.

Since I was too early, the chateau not yet being open to visitors, I made my way down the avenue of planes and sat under one of the trees. I thought of certain resemblances behind the story of Oswald and Corinne.

Oswald and Corinne, in their outward personae at least. reminded me of another pair of famous lovers; Nelson and Lady Hamilton. Corinne's improvisations suggest Lady Hamilton's famous "attitudes" (poses imitating scenes, mainly tragic, from classical mythology); and Corinne's dress and demeanor--her extravagant passions, her exotic beauty, her exaggerated gestures, not to mention her ample figure--remind us of Emma Hamilton. Oswald's reserve, his knightly boldness in action and his military career in the West Indies resemble Nelson's. And there is the scene in which their love is set, Naples, Posilipo--there, at the culmination of their six months of happiness, Oswald promised to love Corinne forever while Corinne, improvising with her lyre at the Cumaean Sibyl's temple, had premonitions that this happiness could not last. And then, at the time Mme de Stael was writing *Corinne*, there was the Battle of Trafalgar and Nelson's death.

As I sat under the tree a woman and a small child walked along the path, a train passed by heading for Geneva, and after that there was silence. One disconnected thought seemed to bump up against another: Oswald and Corinne; Nelson and Emma; Posilipo; the Bay of Naples. I seemed to be at the Villa Emma as I remembered it, hearing voices from the terrace and the faint sound of waves below. In the library of the villa books are piled high on the table and marble emperors look down, not disdainful or angry but tired, so tired. Easier to imagine Sir William there than Emma with her maimed hero. Then I thought of that red brick country house in Sussex, my first boarding school, Ashfold. The house had, long before it became a school, been the home of Nelson and Emma's child, Horatia.

Emma Hart came to London from rural Wales. At first engaged as a nurserymaid, her luscious beauty (later depicted obsessively by Romney) gave her the means of escape. She became the mistress of Sir Harry Featherstonehaugh who installed her at Uppark, in Sussex. But Emma was flighty and when she became pregnant Sir Harry (who was not the father) threw her out. She appealed for protection to the Hon Charles Greville. Greville was the young man who, as previously noted, had kept his uncle, Sir William Hamilton, Ambassador in Naples, informed about the scandal surrounding Sir William's friend William Beckford. Greville rented a cottage for Emma and her mother off the Edgware Road.

Greville, like his uncle, was an ardent collector. Unlucky investments, and extravagant expenditure, forced Greville to economize, so he sold his art collection and got rid of his mistress, passing her on to Sir William, by then a widower, who was thirty years older than Emma. While Emma seems to have genuinely loved Greville she adapted herself to her situation and in Naples became celebrated for her beauty and accomplishments, though English visitors sneered at her provincial accent. Sir William came to adore her and eventually asked the Bourbon King for permission to marry his "gallery of statues," as Horace Walpole called her. Romney painted his last portrait of her, this time as Ambassadress, the final sitting on the day of her marriage, 6th September 1791.

Prophetically, shortly before this last portrait of Emma, Romney had painted her as Calypso, the enchantress and beguiler of seafarers. And so, enter Nelson, the naval hero, and the grand passion of their lives.

Horatia was conceived in 1800 aboard the storm-tossed *HMS Foudroyant* as Nelson bore the Hamiltons away from Naples together with the Bourbon Queen. She was born back in England. Nelson and Lady Hamilton pretended Horatia was the daughter of a Navy officer, adopted by them. The strange trio, the Hamiltons and Nelson, were feted everywhere; honor paid to the victor of the Nile. They were even entertained at Fonthill. Though Beckford was ostracized by all the Wiltshire gentry he remained on friendly terms with Sir William, though he came to detest Emma. For the occasion of their visit Beckford devised a "monastic fete" in his new Abbey. Outdoors, in the gloom of a December evening, musicians played and flambeaux were placed among the trees. Indoors the stairs were lit by torches held by "certain mysterious living figures...dressed in hooded gowns." A feast of monastic austerity was served but, to the relief of the guests, a more conventional meal was provided later.

Nelson's sensational Trafalgar victory, and the circumstances of his death, led Parliament to make generous grants to Nelson's family, including a peerage for his brother William and grants of money to his sisters Susanna Bolton and Catherine Matcham. Nothing came to Lady Hamilton or Horatia, either from the state or from Nelson's family. This was despite the provisions of the codicil Nelson made to his will just before his last battle and within sight of the enemy fleets, written in his note book and witnessed by his captains. He wrote: "I leave Emma, Lady Hamilton...a legacy to my King and Country that they will give her an ample provision to maintain her rank in life. I also leave to the beneficence of my country my adopted daughter Horatia...these are the only favors I ask of my King and Country, at this moment, when I am going to fight their battle."

Emma's pleas for money were ignored. Always extravagant, she entertained lavishly, showing off Horatia as the daughter of the great hero. Gradually she sank deeper into debt. She drank heavily and put on weight. She was given to furious rages. Forced by her debts into a sponging house she entertained guests there in a delusional manner which inevitably puts one in mind of Mr Dorrit at the Marshalsea. Finally, deserted by everyone, her resources at an end, she fled to Calais to escape her creditors. There she and Horatia lived in mean lodgings, with Horatia sleeping in an alcove in her mother's bedroom. Horatia sat with her mother as she sank into delirium. Horatia later described the horror of those days. Her mother "took little interest in anything but the indulgence of her unfortunate habit" (that is, "spirits and wine to a fearful degree.") Horatia never left her mother's room. "For some time before she died," she added, "she was not kind to me, but she had much to try her...and I was too well aware of the state of her finances..." Horatia did write with some generosity of feeling that for all Emma's faults ("and she had many") she had fine qualities which "had she been placed early in better hands, would have made her a very superior woman." From this it may be assumed that Horatia had a pretty clear idea of Emma's raffish early history.

Lady Hamilton died in January 1815 and was buried at Calais. Horatia returned to England and came to live at Ashfold with the Matchams. At fourteen she was no longer a child. The two years she had spent confined in squalid lodgings with her desperate and dissipated--and dying--mother had left their mark. Her miniature portrait by Richard Cosway, done shortly after her return to England, shows her with dark eyes seemingly too large for her pale face. Evidently she had suffered. As she wrote, "at the death of Lady Hamilton I was but fourteen--true, but circumstances form an almost child's character into that of a woman and that was unfortunately my case...Alas...the time I spent in Calais is too indelibly stamped on my memory ever to forget." One consequence of these experiences was her refusal to accept that Emma could have been her mother; or perhaps it was a simple refusal to believe that the great patriotic hero could have been an adulterer living in the same house with Emma's complaisant husband, Sir William.

Mrs Matcham had bought Ashfold Lodge in 1807 with the government grant made after Nelson's death. When Horatia arrived the Matchams had nine children (four others had died previously). It seems to have been a happy household. In 1822 Horatia married a clergyman, Philip Ward, by whom she had nine children. She died in 1881.

*   *   *

Ashfold must have looked much the same when I came to it as a schoolboy after the War as it did when Horatia arrived there in 1815. The house sat on terraced lawns with a view, beyond the ha-ha, of the South Downs. There were beech woodlands and, a short walk away, a lake where we swam on warm summer days. The paneled library had bound past numbers of Punch and the Illustrated London News. The school has since moved and I am told the house has been torn down to make way for housing developments.

Ashfold was not a particularly convenient school, since we lived near Oxford and it was an awkward drive. When I arrived in England after the War I was too ignorant to go to any school, but after a year of the indifferent tutoring I have already described, my father decided that the time had come, however inadequately prepared I might be. One day he showed me a few boarding school prospectuses and the letters from the headmasters which accompanied them. He asked me to read them and tell him which one I preferred, as if the decision was entirely mine. I picked out Ashfold. He asked me why. I said that the headmaster had sent the prospectus with a handwritten note that seemed to reveal a congenial character and contained a personal invitation to visit the school, rather than the usual form letter typed by a secretary. I don't know if my reason for my choice impressed my father but he went along with it. The Ashfold Headmaster, James Harrison (who much later explained the handwritten letter by saying his secretary had been ill) had taken his school to Canada during the War and probably struck my father, for this reason, as being more likely than the others to be understanding of an American child, even one as backward as myself. Anyway, to Ashfold I was sent.

I was happy at Ashfold, despite my struggles with Latin and Mathematics. Two memories asserted themselves and rose above the others, my arrival there and my departure. The excitement of going away to school was stimulated by the long and detailed list of items required: shirts, shorts, sports clothes, right down to sponge bag and the Book of Common Prayer, each to be labeled with my name and school number. Assembling all this sometimes required trips to London, which meant that, once the school shopping had been done, I could go off with my mother for a delicious tea or a matinee performance at the theatre. Finally the day arrived when all these preparations found their fulfillment. I was taken to school by car, though subsequently at the beginning of term I would travel by train to be met on arrival at the local station along with the other boys on the same train. On that first day, as my parents drove down the drive to the school, between dense clumps of trees, any feeling of eager anticipation or boyish bravado I may have had vanished and gave way to foreboding as I realized that I was about to enter a different world to any I had previously known. The feeling will be familiar to many. As my parents' car disappeared down the drive

I ducked into the woods to compose my features and wipe away the unmanly tears. Months later I was looking through the bound volumes of Punch in the school library and found a cartoon of the 1920's. It may have been my first discovery of the healing power of absurdity. A father, sending his small son to boarding school, consoles him: "I know what you feel old man. I felt the same when I left for the front in the War." The boy replies: "Yes, but you had a revolver."

I left Ashfold in a more dramatic fashion. Towards the end of my last term, which was a summer term, I started feeling pains in my legs. At first these symptoms were dismissed as "growing pains" comparable, I suppose, to the time when, in the middle of my reading the lesson in chapel, my voice suddenly broke and moved from a boyish treble to an inarticulate grunting cough, to my embarrassment and the delight of the assembled boys. But the pains in my legs persisted and I was put in bed and an outside doctor was called in to advise. The result was panic among the school staff, perceptible even to me tucked up in bed in the school sanatorium. In those pre-Salk days polio, as it was called, or sometimes Infantile Paralysis, was a recurrent terror to parents. Every summer, it seemed, some swimming pool would be closed to children in the wake of a polio scare. No sooner was I diagnosed with polio than the Headmaster decided to close the school and send all the boys home. Luckily, it was near the end of term.

I shall never forget my mother's arrival to fetch me from school. She drove the car herself. My father was away, in Australia I believe, on a business trip. On the back seat of the car my mother had placed a blanket and a thermos flask of iced water. I was to lie down on the back seat as she drove. While her face, taught with fear, was disturbing, I was too delighted see her again and to be going home to have much anxiety at the cause of it. My chatter on the way must have been a torment to her, with her thoughts full of fear of crippling paralysis. But she kept up a cheerful appearance as best she could.

I was not actually going home but was on my way to the Oxford Isolation Hospital where I was to spend the rest of the summer in a room to which no one was admitted except for the nurse who brought me my food and the books provided by my parents and their friends. Strangely, I was no longer in any great pain and boredom and loneliness were the worst things I suffered that summer--with occasional interludes of fear brought on by the uncertainty of my condition and the taciturnity of the hospital staff; no one told me anything, even when they drew fluid from my spine. There were occasions when I would be brought to a window to see my parents and my sister waving to me outside.

I became friendly with the nurse who would talk to me sometimes about the books I was reading. Apart from that she seemed mainly concerned that I was eating enough. I had no appetite and the food was not appealing--hospital food rarely is, and this was England in the immediate post War in which relentlessly boiled potatoes were standard fare. I found them particularly inedible. Not wishing to annoy the nurse I dumped some of them in the drawer of the bedside table. A few weeks later, when I was about to leave the hospital, I opened the drawer. There was a scuttling of black beetles about the remains of the potatoes. I closed the drawer and left.

XIII

Mme De Stael -- Benjamin Constant

Entering the Coppet chateau through the courtyard, the entrance gates of which front a narrow road and the park, I was met by a red-haired Irish girl who acted as guardian and guide, though I was left to wander through the rooms unaccompanied. The place has the feeling of a family house. There are many pictures of Mme de Stael and her family and friends.

Jacques Necker settled permanently at Coppet after his wife died, at Beaulieu near Lausanne, in 1794. At the chateau there is a drawing of her on her deathbed with the inscription, in English, "Not lost but gone before." A pastel portrait made from this drawing shows her wearing a white headdress adorned with ribbons. The frame bears the words "He will love me forever." These inscriptions bear witness to the cult of Mme Necker's memory to which her husband devoted himself after her death—a death which she anticipated with morbid obsessiveness—probably out of a sense of guilt, for in later life she became cold and assumed a rigid Calvinist piety. There is another portrait of her at the chateau, painted when she was forty-four, by Duplessis, showing her in a dress of rich white satin with a bodice covered with small bows. Her hair is powdered. She is clearly the wife of a very rich man and the mistress of an intellectual salon. She once described herself as having a "tall and well proportioned figure, though lacking that enchanting elegance which increases its value," and presenting herself with "a country air." This seems frank, but is probably deceptive.

She was born Susan Curchod, the daughter of a Protestant minister in a Swiss mountain village. She met Edward Gibbon in Lausanne. In June 1757 Gibbon wrote in his journal: "I saw Mademoiselle Curchod--omnia vincit amor, et nos caedamus amori." Gibbon admired not only her beauty but also her erudition. He found her "learned without pedantry, lively in conversation, pure in sentiment, and elegant in manners." She welcomed his suit, which was encouraged by her parents. But Gibbon's father would not hear of this marriage and threatened to cut Gibbon off if he persisted in it, leaving him destitute. Gibbon yielded to his fate. "I sighed as a lover, I obeyed as a son." Mlle Curchod became a teacher in Geneva and in due course met and married Jacques Necker. Gibbon never again thought seriously about marrying. Rousseau thought that Mlle Curchod would not have been happy with a man of such a cold temperament as Gibbon, and he was probably right. Jacques Necker was undoubtedly a better bargain. Money aside, he was better looking--Gibbon was very ugly. Gibbon remained on friendly terms with both Neckers and saw them often in Paris and Geneva; he was even able to assist them, and Mme de Stael, in the tumultuous period of the Revolution and the Terror in France.

Needless to say, the chateau also contains many memorials to the beloved father of Mme de Stael, including his full length white marble statue, showing him draped in a toga *a l'antique*, which Mme de Stael commissioned from a German sculptor. It is dated 1817, the year of her own death. It welcomes the visitor in the entrance hall.

The great days of Mme de Stael's reign at Coppet began in 1804 and 1805 when she was writing *Corinne*. Much as she loved the place it felt to her a bit like a prison, exiled as she was from Paris where she hoped to play a political role. As punishment for her outspoken opposition, Napoleon placed her under an edict of banishment; she was forbidden to approach within forty leagues of Paris. The extent of the Emperor's resentment, and his fear of her intrigues, seems extraordinary. Over a period of five months, in 1806 and 1807, in the midst of his bloodiest campaigns and despite the pressure of other business, he wrote ten letters to Fouché alone on the subject of Mme de Stael, warning him not to allow "that hussy" near Paris.

While enduring this banishment Mme de Stael gathered around her a devoted and obedient group of intellectuals--Sismondi, Bonstetten, Schlegel--and, of course, Benjamin Constant, now (together with Chateaubriand and Mme Recamier) the best known of those who frequented the chateau in those years.

Life at the chateau was like an informal but continuous seminar fitfully conducted by a tyrant. Mme de Boigne left a description of the *vie de chateau* in those days: "Life at Coppet was strange. It seemed as leisurely as it was unstructured. There were no rules; no one had the slightest idea where they were to be or to meet. There was no place specially designed for a particular time of day. Everybody's rooms were open. One simply pitched one's tent wherever a discussion began, and there one would remain for hours, for days, without the interruption of any of the ordinary habits of life. Discussion seemed to be everybody's chief occupation. And yet, everyone was engaged in serious work...Mme de Stael worked very hard, but when she had nothing better to do, she was always ready for the slightest social pleasure. She adored acting, shopping, excursions, entertaining people, going to visit them, but first and foremost she loved to talk."

Everyone who ever met Germaine de Stael mentioned her volubility and love of good talk. There is one other version of the myth of the Cumaean Sybil, which Turner made the subject of a painting, but of which Mme de Stael may have been ignorant--or she may have chosen to ignore it. In this story Apollo agreed to grant the Sybil a wish. She asked to live as many years as the number of grains of sand she could hold in her hand. The wish was granted, but the Sybil was given only the longevity she asked for, not freedom from aging. After many years she wasted away to nothing--all that remained was her inextinguishable voice.

What Mme de Boigne omits to mention is the extent to which all these discussions and activities were dominated by the hostess herself. While her intelligence and love of discussion are well attested, by others as well as Mme de Boigne; less so her absolute sway over her circle and the psychological tyranny she exercised. Also, the lack of any privacy must have been maddening. Benjamin Constant wrote in his journal (1804): "I am interrupted at every moment. Oh Solitude! Solitude! more necessary to my talent even than to my happiness! I like everything to do with Coppet, but all those people, all those incessant interruptions, exhaust me and get on my nerves. They drain my natural energy and force me to exclaim with some bitterness--'When will it all end?'" Mme de Stael would bustle about the house noisily at all hours, invading every bedroom, interrupting all conversation, armed with a green morocco writing case in which she would inscribe her thoughts, dressed in turbans of emerald and scarlet, trailing scarves of purple and gold.

Walking through the chateau now one gets only the faintest suggestion of this atmosphere. The gallery, where plays were performed--the French classics as well as Mme de Stael's own play, *Agar in the Desert*--is now the library, a tranquil room with French windows opening onto a terrace with a view of the lake. The house has been altered in other respects. Mme de Stael's upstairs suite of rooms was converted into a chapel by her great-granddaughter, but some of Mme de Stael's bedroom furniture remains in the house, including her magnificent bed with its carved cupids above the canopy. Prophetic, in a sense, is the drawing of the young Germaine Necker, at the age of fourteen, in a full-skirted dress with a tightly-laced waist, her hair dressed in the voluminous style of the late eighteenth century. Already a participant in the discussions at her mother's Paris salon, the child has her mouth half open as if about to interject an observation of precocious perspicacity.

There is a small portrait of Benjamin Constant at Coppet. Though doubtless flattering, it shows him as one imagines him to have been in life--red haired, not handsome, quizzical, humorous, intelligent, with a slightly mad glint in his eye. In *The Red Notebook*, an autobiography of his early life, and *Adolphe*, the novel based on his affair with Mme de Stael, he exposed himself in all his moral and emotional frailty. Like Rousseau in his *Confessions* he appeared to defy ridicule and contempt. And yet, walking through the rooms of Coppet, I could not entirely separate my image of Mme de Stael from what I knew of this obsessive, exalted, bitter, productive, passionate and tormented relationship.

*   *   *

Constant was born in Lausanne. He was a year younger than Mme de Stael. His mother died shortly after his birth. His father, Col Juste de Constant, served with a regiment of Swiss mercenaries, posted in various garrison towns. Benjamin was entrusted to a series of tutors each of whom was either vicious, dishonest, mad or simply incompetent. The first of these, however, did him a service. He persuaded the boy that they should invent a private language, which turned out to be Greek, and Benjamin was fluent by the time he was five. Col Juste took Benjamin to Oxford but was disappointed to discover that, at thirteen, he was too young to be enrolled in the University; so he sent him to the University at Erlangen, in Germany, then to Edinburgh where he studied for a year and a half. By 1786 Benjamin, then nineteen, was in Paris leading a dissolute life devoted mainly to compulsive gambling, and was deeply in debt.

It was then that he met one of the two women who were to have enormous influence over him. Mme de Charriere was Dutch, born at the family castle of Zuylen. She had been known as Belle de Zuylen, or Zélide. Her story has been brilliantly told by Geoffrey Scott in his *Portrait of Zélide*. She was clever, witty, educated--qualities which tended to impede rather than assist her desire to marry and escape the suffocating correctness of her family home. She struck up a romantic friendship with the Seigneur d'Hermanches, but he was already married. He, helpfully, tried to arrange a marriage for her with his friend the Comte de Bellegarde. Though Zélide never loved Bellegarde, he was suitable; but he backed off. With his turgid temperament he could not face the prospect of so much wit and intellectual challenge. Next, she considered the young Scot, James Boswell, a law student at Utrecht. But he had his own ideas of an ideal wife, dutiful and submissive, consonant with the feudal pretensions with which he tried to impress his elderly London friend, Samuel Johnson. Another possible suitor was Lord Wemyss, attainted leader of the Jacobite rebellion of 1745. But he was dissolute and violent and offended Zélide's father with his demands for a marriage settlement. So Zélide found herself on the shelf at twenty-eight, an age which at that time was perilously close to a sentence of spinsterhood. In desperation she married her brother's tutor, the worthy but dull Swiss M de Charriere, and went with him to live at his family manor of Colombier, near Neuchatel. There she found a senile father-in-law, two malicious sisters-in-law, and utter boredom. She had a brief and disastrous love affair with a young man in Geneva, and a nervous breakdown. She treated herself with opium and dealt with the love affair and consequent depression in a novel, *Caliste*, which she said she never had the courage to re-read; "…it cost me too many tears to write." Charriere's remedy was to take his wife to Paris. There she met Benjamin Constant, the nephew of her old confidant d'Hermanches.

While Benjamin was twenty-seven years younger than Zélide he was just what her starved appetite for intellectual novelty and stimulation required. As for Benjamin, "the turn of her mind delighted me," he wrote long afterwards; "we spent whole days and nights in talk. She was very severe in her judgements on everything that surrounded her. My own nature was full of mockery. We suited each other perfectly.." He found her outlook on life "so original and lively, her contempt for conventional prejudices so profound, her intellect so forceful, her superiority to average human nature so vigorous and assured, that for me, a boy of twenty, as eccentric and scornful as herself, her company was a joy such as I had never yet known. I gave myself up to it rapturously."

What, exactly, did Mme de Charriere see in this boy? He had an impulsive, scapegrace quality which was amusing enough to be sure, but added to it a critical mind and a fluent tongue. He could do crazy things, but then examine why he had done them and laugh at his own folly. He had, above all, an openness to experience, however imprudent, and a belief that even unfortunate experiences could be redeemed by a sense of the ridiculous.

In one such episode Benjamin convinced himself he should marry an heiress, Mlle Pourrat. But she was betrothed to another. He wrote passionate letters suggesting they elope, which Mlle Pourrat dutifully showed to her mother. For whatever reason, the mother allowed Benjamin to continue to see her and her daughter, even though Benjamin continued his letters to the daughter (who was in no way attracted to him). Mme Pourrat's lover misconstrued these meetings and there was a jealous scene. Overcome by the absurdity of his position, Benjamin staged a suicide attempt. He produced a bottle of Mme de Charriere's opium which he attempted to drink. The bottle was knocked from his hand. At this point Mlle Pourrat entered dressed for the opera and, forgetting suicide, Benjamin accompanied her to the first performance of *Tartare* by Beaumarchais.

On another occasion Benjamin was summoned by his father to Bois-le-Duc where Juste was stationed. A lieutenant was sent to bring in the prodigal. Benjamin gave the lieutenant the slip, spent the night with a prostitute he knew, and headed for England with nothing more than a few Louis and a spare shirt. In England he travelled alone, mainly on horseback, looked up people he had met or heard of, borrowed money. He bought two dogs and a monkey. (He did not get on with the monkey and traded it for another dog.) Leaving London he rode north, through the Midlands and

Cumbria, and reached Edinburgh where he met old University friends.

Benjamin was away for some three months. His father implored him to return, saying his health was threatened by worry. Benjamin headed for Dover, his only remaining dog collapsing on the way, exhausted. Reaching Bois-le-Duc he feared his father's reproaches. Instead he found his father playing cards with some officers. "Ah, so it is you," he said. "You must be tired...Go to bed." The next day his father saw Benjamin's coat was torn and said "That's just what I always feared would come of this trip." No other words passed between them on the subject. Benjamin had hoped for at least some discussion of his difficulties and motives, some reconciliation and forgiveness. But in place of intimacy there was silence. Perhaps what he took for indifference was really concealed resentment; but, "on this occasion, as on a thousand others during my life, I was halted by a shyness that I have never been able to overcome, and my words died on my lips as soon as I saw no encouragement to continue." I think it probable that father and son simply could not understand one another, to the extent they found no common language in which even to express their incomprehension. It must be said, though, that Juste, though he might have been reticent and shy, was also very strange. Before he married Benjamin's mother he had taken a fancy to a nine-year-old girl he saw in Lausanne. He abducted the girl, took her to Holland, educated her, and in due time made her his mistress and, eventually, his wife. Benjamin was unaware of this stepmother until he was in his twenties, when he was shocked to discover that she had given him a half-brother and sister.

On his way to his father's house in Lausanne Benjamin stopped off at Neuchatel, and there Mme de Charriere received him "with transports of joy." It is here that the memoir effectively ends.

Benjamin settled in happily at Colombier where he started work on his massive *History of Religion* and had long conversations, sometimes lasting through the night, with Mme de Charriere. What did they talk about, at first around the stove and then, when she had retired, at her bed? "How happy we were." he wrote, "discussing the relation between genius and insanity." Whatever the topic for discussion, they played off one another; he with his eccentric visions and she with her sarcasms, her opinion that human conventions were either stupid or cruel. Their love affair, for such one may call it whatever their sexual relations may have been, lasted for almost ten years, with one interruption.

In 1788 Juste packed Benjamin off to the Court at Brunswick where he had arranged a place for him as a junior Chamberlain. There, in a typically confused and impulsive way, Benjamin married one of the ladies of the court, Baroness Minna von Cramm. He found her weeping and took pity on her. She was lonely and not very attractive, and nine years older than Benjamin. After a few months they separated and were soon divorced. Minna retired with her menagerie which, in 1813, consisted of 120 birds, two squirrels, six cats, eight dogs and assorted crows, fish, etc--all living together in one squalid room.

Benjamin returned gratefully to Colombier and Mme de Charriere and their talks late into the night.

But, of course, this could not last. By 1794 Benjamin, though still erratic and impulsive, was not the youth he was in 1788. Mme de Charriere had shared responsibility for his early escapades. She had, "by ceaselessly entertaining me with the stupidity of the human species and the absurdity of prejudices, and by sharing my admiration for all that was fantastical, extraordinary and original...ended by inspiring me with a veritable thirst to find myself, too, beyond the human pale." This was the mocking tone of eighteenth century comedy, of Beaumarchais, even of *commedia del arte* farce. The French Revolution rendered all that obsolete. Mme de Charriere's rational scepticism, her ironic wit, her constant negations, her eighteenth century cast of mind generally, now seemed to Benjamin limited, unserious. Benjamin was restless. Benjamin was ready for heroic engagement, the violent charge of Romanticism. This arrived in the form of Mme de Stael.

Mme de Stael came to see Mme de Charriere at Colombier, as an admirer of *Caliste*. She said she had read it ten times. The author was not impressed. She reported to Benjamin: "She boasted of her wits as if she had none. She boasted of her titled friends as if her husband had picked her up the day before in a milliner's shop. She boasted of the great world of Paris as if she had been a girl from the provinces who had only been there six weeks...What fun we shall have discussing her."

Benjamin was undeterred. In September he rode up to Coppet. Being told by the servants that Mme de Stael had left an hour before, he galloped after her carriage and caught up with it just outside Nyon. She invited him to join her in the carriage. They immediately entered into a serious conversation on the freedom of the press. At Rolle, where she was to attend a dinner, Mme de Stael asked Benjamin to join her. The conversation started that evening was to continue for fifteen years.

Benjamin wrote to Mme de Charriere that his life was changed. Now he looked forward with excited hope. As for Mme de Stael: "I have seldom seen such a combination of astonishing and attractive qualities; so much brilliance together with so much truth, such expansive but also positive goodness, such immense generosity, such sweet and sustained politeness in society, so much charm and simplicity; such a total naturalness with her intimate friends... she feels other people's intelligence with as much pleasure as her own. She brings out those she loves with an amazing and constant attention which demonstrates in her as much goodness as wit. In short, she is a being apart, a superior being such as one might come across once in a hundred years..." To this effusiveness he added, coyly: "This is the second woman in my life who could be all the world to me, who could be a whole universe in herself. You know who was the first." Mme de Charriere was not deceived. She knew she was beaten.

*   *   *

Benjamin Constant moved into Coppet and soon made it known that it was not only the conversation of Mme de Stael that attracted him. He declared his passion for her, which she rebuffed. He was not physically attractive, with his lanky red hair, blotchy skin (probably the result of syphilis) and inflamed eyes. Mme de Stael was no beauty herself, but she found him repulsive, though she enjoyed his company and his talk. But Constant would not give up. He even tried his old trick of pretended suicide. One night the house was aroused by shrieks coming from his room. He was found writhing in agony with the empty opium bottle beside him. "It is for you that I perish," he gasped seizing Mme de Stael's arm and covering it with kisses. She implored him to live. "If you command it I will try," he said, and recovered immediately. Back in her room Mme de Stael washed the arm he had so ardently kissed in perfumed water, telling a friend that Constant revolted her.

Eventually, Constant's passionate approaches were rewarded. He worked closely with Mme de Stael on political matters in Switzerland and in Paris during the Directoire period, and by 1796 they had become lovers. The text is still preserved of the compact they entered into that year to "dedicate our lives to each other..." They regarded themselves as "indissolubly bound" to one another, their destiny in every sense a "common destiny." Constant added a codicil of his own: "I declare that it is from the very bottom of my heart that I enter into this engagement; that I know nothing on earth so adorable as Mme de Stael...that I regard it as the greatest good fortune of my life to be able to render her youth happy, to grow old gently by her side, and to reach the final bourne in company with one who understands me and without whom nothing on this earth would be worth while."

In June 1797 Mme de Stael's daughter Albertine, later to become Duchesse de Broglie, was born in Paris. Although Mme de Stael's estranged husband, the Baron de Stael, pretended the child was his, many knew otherwise; and Albertine's red hair, so evident in the portrait of Albertine and her mother by Mme Vigee-Lebrun at Coppet, testifies to Constant's parentage.

In 1802 the Baron de Stael died, and Constant felt obliged to ask Mme de Stael to marry him. To his relief, she refused. She did not wish, she explained, to exchange a name she had made famous for that of an unknown. By 1803 their relationship was becoming less and less happy. Her incessant demands made it impossible for him to get on with his work, the interminable *History of Religion.* "Never," he wrote in his journal, "have I met a woman who is so incessantly exacting. One's whole life (every minute, every hour, every year) must be at her disposal. When she gets into one of her rages, then it is a tumult of all the earthquakes and typhoons rolled into one..." There was a "frightful scene" which lasted until three in the morning. She said that he "lacked sensibility," that he "did not deserve to be trusted," but the real problem seemed to be his waning ardor. "I don't enjoy," he wrote, "being scolded by a woman whose youth is leaving her. I do not enjoy being asked to make love, after ten years of a love affair [ie, since 1794 when they met], when each of us is approaching forty years of age and when I had told her two hundred times, and ages ago, that I had done with passion..I must detach my life from hers while remaining her friend; otherwise I shall not survive much longer." But how to do this? "It is terrible," he wrote "the relationship between a man who has ceased to love and a woman who does not wish to cease being loved. As always the idea of losing me makes Germaine value me more; a long habit of disposing of my entire existence, makes her forever sure that I must come back to her...as I truly love her, the pain she feels when she does not find in me the feelings she desires, causes me intense pain." Her distress following the death of her father made it even more difficult for him to escape. Her demands were greater than ever--she insisted on long discussions in the middle of the night. "One must obey," he wrote. "It is impossible to explain the dominance she establishes..." There were more reproaches and rages.

In 1805 Constant was in Paris and too busy to write in his journal every day so he devised a number code which he used for several years. Frequently arising situations could thus be indicated with maximum economy of time. The code:

1. Physical [ie, sexual] pleasure.
2. Desire to break my eternal chain [with Mme de Stael].
3. Reconciliation with this bond, because of memories or a momentary charm.
4. Work.
5. Disputes with my father.
6. Tenderness for my father.

And so on through number 13 ("Indecision about everything") to number 17: Desire to make up with certain enemies [ie, Napoleon].

In July, after receiving a letter from Mme de Stael, he was prompted to write fourteen 2's in a row; but he left for Coppet.

In January 1807 Constant entered a New Year's Resolution in his diary: "I must put an end to all this. She is the most selfish, demented, ungrateful, empty and vindictive of women. Why did I not break with her long ago? She is odious to me, unendurable. I shall die if I do not bring the thing to an end..." The only means of escape seemed to be through marriage. As he wrote to his Swiss cousin, "Obviously I must marry, if only to get to bed at a reasonable hour."

Constant turned to an old flame, Charlotte von Hardenberg, with whom he had had an affair in Germany in 1793. She was now married, but he persuaded her to divorce her husband. Constant and Charlotte were married in 1808 while Mme de Stael was safely in Austria. When Mme de Stael returned to Coppet she resumed her old domination, such that he did not dare to reveal his marriage. For over a year Constant kept his marriage secret, remaining at Coppet without seeing Charlotte. In a letter he confessed, and excused, his duplicity: "... when the truth is certain to cause pain, then it is pride, not duty, which forces one to tell it...True morality consists in avoiding, so far as one can, the infliction of suffering." Finally Charlotte came to Switzerland and confronted Mme de Stael. Mme de Stael threw herself at Constant's feet, uttering "terrible cries of anguish and desolation..." He pleaded that "A heart of iron could not have resisted. So I have returned to Coppet with her...Oh God, what can I do? I am trampling on my future and my happiness." Charlotte then attempted suicide, taking poison. An antidote was administered and she recovered. She threatened to try again unless Constant came to her. Mme de Stael threatened to stab herself if he did, and even tried unsuccessfully to strangle herself. Constant remained a prisoner at Coppet.

It was only in 1811 that the chains were broken when Mme de Stael fell in love with a dashing, and much younger, cavalry officer, John Rocca, whom she eventually married. Rocca was smitten with love for her. There is a portrait of Rocca at Coppet, handsome in his hussar's uniform, standing alongside his black charger, Sultan, the horse he trained to kneel before her window as a token of the devotion of his master to the mistress of Coppet. Rocca challenged Constant to a duel, which Mme de Stael prevented. The spell, though, was broken and Constant escaped to Germany with his wife. He did not return to Switzerland for thirteen years.

*   *   *

Leaving the chateau I found the weather had changed. The sky darkened as the clouds rolled in, followed by thunder and flashes of lightning. The waves on the lake turned grey/green and the swans gleamed stark white against the darkening water. The flags at the landing stage snapped in the wind. Soon the rain came lashing down. I took shelter in a cafe while I waited for the steamer to Geneva.

While there I finished reading Constant's short novel, *Adolphe*, which he wrote in two weeks in 1807, In it he revealed all the shame and frustration he had felt in the face of the claims of his exacting mistress. The details of the life and person of the mistress in the novel were suggested by Anne Lindsay, a woman with whom Constant had had an affair in 1800, but there can be no doubt that the difficulties he narrator has in breaking with Ellénore, as Constant calls her, were a record of Constant's entanglement with Mme de Stael. When Constant read the novel to Mme de Stael she was furious and made a tempestuous scene; the sort of scenes, as Constant wrote in his journal, which "cause me physical pain. I coughed blood." Byron in 1816 reported that Mme de Stael was angered by the suggestion that the novel was about her--after all, Ellénore was described as being unintelligent!--but no one was fooled.

The narrator, Adolphe, describes himself at the outset as a part-time student who, in the way of young men, wanted to be loved though he had no marked preference for anyone. He meets Ellénore, the mistress of a nobleman, by whom she has two children, and sets out to conquer her. Suddenly, the love which he had feigned seized him with frenzy. Ellénore's resistance only inflames his desire. At last she yields; his passionate outbursts "frightened her to a submissiveness, a tenderness and an idolatrous veneration."

Adolphe gives himself to the joys of love but, while Ellénore was a source of pleasure in his life, "she no longer represented a goal; she had become a bond." He counseled restraint, but if he stayed away this apparent indifference caused her pain, which led in turn to a fever of remorse on his part which sent him running back to her. Love was now mingled with guilt.

Things become worse when Ellénore, out of love for Adolphe, leaves her aristocratic protector and abandons her children. This unasked for sacrifice, and the loss of freedom it entails, is a burden too heavy for his love, and Adolphe reflects: "It is a fearful misfortune not to be loved when you love; but it is a much greater misfortune to be loved passionately when you love no longer."

Adolphe, like Constant, lacks the courage, or the cruelty, to break off the affair. Ellénor, who is Polish, returns to Poland and Adolphe follows her. There he sinks deeper into the vortex of a doomed relationship, bringing him only a life "devoid of courage, full of discontent and humiliation." He procrastinates, hoping to end it in a way "gentler and more tender with her in order to preserve at least memories of friendship." But, of course, this is impossible. Once rejected, Ellénore declines into a fatal illness. She dies, saying: "I wanted what was impossible. Love was all my life: it could not be all yours."

Adolphe, at the end, conscious of having broken the heart of "the being I loved...that companion heart to mine which...had persisted in devoting itself to me," goes on to live in solitude "in this desert of a world which I had so often wished to cross independently."

This summary of the plot does no justice to the passages, painfully delineated, describing the psychological torments--erotic love, regret, resentment, guilt, anger--endured by the protagonists. Adolphe, wrote Byron, "is a work which leaves an unpleasant impression, but very consistent with the consequences of not being in love, which is, perhaps, as disagreeable as anything, except being so." This is witty, but too facile. In a heightened way the story explores the dilemma, all too common, which arises when passion flags, as inevitably it must. At this pitch the emotion is usually more transitory in a man than in a woman, as Byron well knew. (He had Julia, abandoned by Don Juan, reflect: "Man's love is of man's life a thing apart, 'Tis woman's whole existence.") Without the cooler emotions and genuine affection the result must be increased demands, apparent servitude, resentment followed by anger and harsh words which cannot be recalled.

134

What is unusual about Adolphe, though, is that, when the transports of love faded in intensity, he felt obliged to substitute for it an exaggerated sense of pity, creating a tormenting conflict between heartlessness and compassion. Thus Adolphe and Ellénore found themselves in an emotional deadlock to which there was no solution but death. One source of this guilt might be Adolphe's awareness that the original emotion of love was at least half feigned. Perhaps Benjamin Constant really was the "vieille cocotte" that Mme Talma, who introduced him to Anne Lindsay, called him. His letters to Anne were, in her view, "a mixture of passion and indifference; of the outspoken and the sly." He wanted to seduce women but could only charm them. Harold Nicolson wrote of Constant that: "For him, love was not so much an emotion kindled by the personality of someone else; it was an ecstasy generated within his own imagination and projected outwards until, almost fortuitously, it encountered some solid object." This suggests that, like his addiction to gambling, love was a drug which provided an acute stimulus to motions of his brain; but, again like a drug, there was a let-down when the quality of the emotion declined. Then followed a desire to escape, which was restrained by pity and the hope, somehow, to redeem the loss. Thus the eighteenth century cult of "feeling" degenerated in Constant to a destructive pathology.

And yet, insofar as the novel reflects the relationship between Constant and Mme de Stael, one wonders. During their long association each found time for other lovers (Anne Lindsay in his case, Count Maurice O'Donnell, among others, in hers). So many of her lovers had tired of her because her demand for love exceeded their capacity. And was not her flamboyant passion, which overwhelmed common sense, a form of selfishness? But, despite her maddening exigencies Constant found intellectual stimulation and real help from her when he needed it. How sincere were Constant's pleas to escape from his bondage to Mme de Stael? Each provided a necessary audience for the other; the connection between them was always theatrical. Constant admits as much in *Adolphe* when, after Ellénore dies, Adolphe reflects: "How much my heart missed that dependence against which I had often rebelled! Formerly, all my actions had an aim; I was sure that each would either spare a pain or cause a pleasure; of this I had complained; I had been irritated that a friendly eye should observe my movements, that the happiness of another should be attached to them. No one now observed them; they interested nobody; no one contended with me for my time nor my hours; no voice called me back when I went out. I was free indeed: I was no longer loved. I was a stranger to all the world."

One senses from this that, for all her demands and hysterics, for all her exaggerations, threats and moral blackmail, Constant needed Mme de Stael, just as she needed him, as the only worthy audience for the ideas and inspirations, and the shrieks and tears, which made up their histrionic relationship.

*   *   *

After his tergiversations during Napoleon's Hundred Days, when he switched from Royalist to Bonapartist and back again, Constant, having lost all credibility as a political figure in France, went to England. He was in Lady Jersey's London drawing room at the same time as Byron in April 1816, just two weeks before Byron's departure for the Continent, but neither recorded the meeting. *Adolphe* was still unpublished, though Constant read it to selected, appreciative audiences. Sometimes both reader and audience were reduced to tears. A diarist wrote of a reading of *Adolphe* in London at this time: "It lasted two hours and a half. The end was so touching, that it was scarcely possible to restrain one's tears, and the effort I made to do so made me positively ill." Constant decided to publish the novel and Caroline Lamb, of all people, sent it to John Murray with a recommendation--"I say it is one of the cleverest things yet written..." Perhaps she admired it as a *roman a clef* in the "kiss and tell" mode of her own *Glenarvon*. Murray turned it down and it was issued by another publisher.

XIV

Summer's End -- and After

It seems strange that Shelley, in his letter to Peacock, has so much to say about his trip to Vevey and Clarens and so little to say of the return from Lausanne. Perhaps, once the Rousseau associations had been exhausted, the rest was an anti-climax. As I leaned over the rail of the steamer I thought that Shelley might have said something about Nyon, a substantial town crowned by an impressive chateau with pepper-pot towers. Originally a Roman settlement for Caesar's retired cavalrymen (Colonia Julia Equestris), the town became the center of a porcelain industry in the late eighteenth century. It may be that, unlike the other small towns on the lake, it had too much of a modern, even industrial, appearance to appeal to Shelley after his earlier raptures in the wilder setting around Vevey.

From Nyon the steamer headed straight across the lake, as Shelley and Byron appear to have done. On the cloudy day of my crossing, a cool day in late August, with the water glassy smooth and the mist hanging low over the mountains, the surface at the middle of the lake was vaporous. As we approached Geneva I could see, above Cologny, a rising plume of smoke signifying the end of summer; someone cleaning up the spent waste of the year's growth.

* * *

The summer of 1816 and the intimate companionship that distinguished it came to an end on August 26th with the arrival of Byron's friends Hobhouse and Scrope Davies, bringing with them the gossip of the London society from which Byron had been estranged. This brought out all Byron's habits of mind and discourse--witty, cynical, cruel--at variance with the Shelleyan mixture of philosophical idealism and reverence for nature which had contributed to the tone of their conversations since the two poets met in June. So the party broke up three days later with the departure of the Shelley entourage for England. Byron proceeded with his friends later through Switzerland and on to Italy. Claire must have been quite evidently pregnant by then--the baby, Allegra, was born the following January. There were no farewell embraces. Byron found Claire an embarrassment and did not wish his friends to see her. She had been copying out for him the Third Canto of *Childe Harold*. She wrote: "It is said that you expressed yourself decisively last evening that it is impossible to see you at Diodati. If you will trust it [the MS] down here [Maison Chapuis] I will take the greatest possible care of it; and finish it in an hour or two. Remember how short a time I have to teize [sic] you and that you will soon be left to your dearly-bought freedom." There was no word from Byron, who watched from an upstairs window at Diodati as the carriage conveying the Shelley party departed along the lakeside.

While Claire may have made herself ridiculous as an over-enthusiastic fan throwing herself at Byron, there is undoubted pathos in her departure as a pregnant, cast-off mistress. She wrote a touching farewell letter to Byron: "When you receive this I shall be miles away; don't be impatient with me. I don't know why I write unless it is because it seems like speaking to you. Indeed I should have been happier if I could have seen you and kissed you once before I went, but now I feel as if we had parted ill friends. You say you will write to me dearest. [He never did.] Do, pray, and be kind in your letters...my dreadful fear is lest you quite forget me--I shall pine through all the wretched winter months whilst you, I hope, may never have one uneasy thought...Farewell, then, dearest, I shall love you to the end of my life and nobody else..."

Byron's indifference had turned to revulsion, but there is something repellent in his cynical dismissal, as he put it in a letter to a friend: "I never loved nor pretended to love her, but a man is a man, and if a girl of eighteen comes prancing to you at all hours there is but one way--the suite of all this is that she was with *child*--and returned to England to assist in peopling that desolate island...is the brat mine? I have reasons to think so, for I know as much as one can know such a thing..."

Poor Byron; for all his appeal to women and his rakish affectations, he seems in almost all his attachments, other than the most fleeting ones, to have ended up being manipulated. Claire's importunities were finally insufferable. Caroline Lamb's tormenting peculiarities had been beyond bearing. Annabella wanted to reform him out of himself. In 1823 he could write: "There never was a man who gave up so much to women, and all I have gained by it has been the character of treating them harshly."

Even Augusta, the beloved Goose, betrayed him. After Byron left England, Annabella kept up a perverse friendship with Augusta, addressing her in their correspondence in terms of tenderest endearment. She tried to coax out of Augusta a confession of the details of her relationship with Byron, also to force her to repudiate him as a form of punishment. From September 1816 Annabella managed to secure Augusta's complete submission, getting her to show Annabella all of Byron's letters and to act on her instructions. Annabella exercised a kind of blackmail, threatening to make details of Augusta's affair with Byron public unless she acted as instructed. Annabella sought, as she said, to "suspend this terror over her, to be used as her future dispositions and conduct may render expedient." Augusta was obedient.

Only Teresa Guiccioli, his last attachment, gave Byron some peace. She was young and innocent and devoted. Her husband was a drawback, but he was generally complaisant and eventually an official (that is, Papal) separation was obtained. Byron readily assumed the role of *cavaliere servente*. He seems to have genuinely loved Teresa, to the extent he could love anyone. Even so, he may have later become a bit restless. Greece, one cannot help but feel, came as a distraction and an escape.

When he came to write *Don Juan* Byron chose as the name of his hero the most famous womanizer of all time. But, as TS Eliot observed in a 1937 essay, Byron's Don Juan, in his relations with women, is not made to appear in any way heroic and always takes the passive role; a "strange passivity that has a curious resemblance to innocence." Byron himself said of his Don Juan that "I am true to Nature in making the advances come from the females." Byron's experience bore this out.

For Shelley, among Byron's women Claire was a special case. She was Shelley's sister-in-law, the companion in many of his adventures and he was fond of her--it seems likely they had even been lovers. Shelley also found antipathetical Byron's raffish, dandified, cynical friends from London. This was exposed in his sonnet, *To Laughter*, which came to light in 1976 in a notebook found in a trunk Scrope Davies had deposited with his bank in 1820 when, having been ruined by gambling, he fled England to escape his creditors. How the notebook came to be in Davies' trunk is a mystery. The sonnet, written out in Mary's hand, reads:

> Thy friends were never mine, thou heartless fiend:
> Silence and solitude and calm and storm,
> Hope, before whose veiled shrine all spirits bend
> In worship, and the rainbow vested form
> Of conscience, that within thy hollow heart
> Can find no throne--the love of such great powers
> Which has requited mine in many hours
> Of loneliness thou ne'er hast felt, depart!
> Thou canst not bear the moon's great eye, thou fearest

A fair child clothed in smiles--aught that is high
Or good or beautiful--Thy voice is dearest
To those who mock at truth and Innocency.
I, now alone, weep without shame to see
How many broken hearts lie bare to thee.

The offense is clear, and it goes right back to the symbolic contest between Julie's rose petals and the acacia leaves from Gibbon's terrace at Lausanne. One can imagine Hobhouse and Davies mocking Shelley's Platonic idealism, his "great powers" and his "high, good and beautiful" as so much sentimental twaddle. But is the "heartless fiend" Byron himself who now appeared to Shelley in his true colors for the first time? Does "thy friends" refer to Davies and Hobhouse? The poem is addressed to Laughter, and Laughter's friends included, without doubt, Byron at this reunion. But there is a personal note, one feels, addressed to Byron himself, if we take the "fair child clothed in smiles" to be a reference to the pregnant and rejected Claire. Claire may have been the subject of jokes at Diodati, led by Byron ("How many broken hearts lie bare to thee.")

*   *   *

Following Shelley's return to England life-changing events came swiftly. Mary's half-sister Fanny committed suicide. Then the abandoned Harriet Shelley was found drowned in the Serpentine. The poor girl was pregnant when she killed herself. When Mary and Shelley married soon after, Shelley lost his suit for custody of his children by Harriet.

As if these events were not depressing enough, Shelley's long revolutionary poem *Laon and Cythna* (published as *The Revolt of Islam*, after cuts to remove passages considered by the publisher to be too offensive) received generally hostile reviews. And then there was the general tone of despair brought about by the failure of the hopes which had been kindled in the early days of the

French Revolution and the economic depression following the Napoleonic wars. Shelley wrote that "gloom and misanthropy have become the characteristics of an age in which we live, the solace of a disappointment that unconsciously finds relief only in the willful exaggeration of its own despair...fiction and poetry have been overshadowed by the same infectious gloom." All of this decided Shelley to leave England--as it would turn out to be, forever--and he and Mary and their children, William and Clara, and Claire and her baby, with a Swiss nurse and another servant, embarked for the continent in March 1818.

The connection with Byron, of course, had not ended, though the closeness of the two poets during that summer of 1816 may have been fading. Time had touched the scenes of that summer. In 1818 Shelley's cousin, Thomas Medwin, visited Montalegre. He found the little boat still anchored in the harbor below the Villa Diodati. It was rotten and half submerged in the water. The Maison Chapuis was empty and already lost in a tangle of undergrowth. But by then Shelley was on his way to Italy, with Claire and her, and Byron's, child.

Allegra, as she had been named at Byron's insistence (the Shelleys had at first called her Alba, their pet name for Byron being Albe) was then, in April 1818, a year and three months old. Byron had agreed to take charge of the child so long as he had no further contact with Claire. Claire had agreed to this, probably thinking that it would be in the best interests of her child. The child would thus be guaranteed a certain social standing which she, as an obscure unmarried mother, could not provide. Byron sent a messenger to bring Allegra, along with the nurse Elise, to Venice, where he was then living, leaving Claire, according to Shelley, feeling "wretchedly disconsolate."

By June Shelley and his extended family were settled into a rented house at Bagni di Lucca. In August Claire, and Shelley, were becoming worried about Allegra. The hubbub at Palazzo Mocenigo, where Byron was living with his mistresses and his menagerie of animals, being clearly unsuitable for a small child, Byron had arranged for her to be taken in by the English Consul-General and his wife. The nurse Elise expressed concerns about the child's health. And then Byron's intentions for the child were obscure, or seemed to Claire and Shelley to be perverse. When Allegra was born Byron had written to Augusta: "I am a little puzzled how to dispose of this new production...but shall probably send for and place it in a Venetian convent--to become a good Catholic--(it may be) a *Nun*-- being a character somewhat wanted in our family." This was only half teasing. Among Byron's objections to Claire having anything to do with the upbringing of the child was that she was "atheistical," like Shelley. Byron professed to be "no enemy" to religion thinking (in 1822) that "people can never have *enough* of religion, if they have any." Despite, or perhaps because of, his early exposure to Calvinism, he would "incline...very much to the Catholic doctrines."

Byron's reputation with children was never good. He once wrote jestingly to Augusta: "I abominate the sight of them so much that I have always had the greatest respect for the character of Herod." (Years later, he was very impatient with Leigh Hunt's unruly brood.) Byron had four children--including Augusta's daughter Medora and the bastard child of a servant girl at Newstead--but had no real connection with them. He seemed to care little for any of them, though he said he missed seeing Ada and invoked her ("sole daughter of my house and heart") in the Third Canto of *Childe Harold.* He expressed confidence in her love and blessed her sweet slumbers "from the mountains where I now respire."

Claire's concern is understandable, and she insisted on going to Venice to see Allegra. Shelley agreed to accompany her. When they got there Byron relented. He agreed to let Claire see her daughter, but was adamant in his refusal to see Claire. He was happy to see Shelley, though, and was pleased to welcome him to Venice. After speaking with Shelley, Byron made arrangements for Claire and

Allegra to spend time together in a villa Byron had rented in the Euganean Hills.

* * *

It was at that meeting in Venice that Shelley and Byron acted out the conclusion of the disagreement first recorded in Lausanne on Gibbon's terrace in the summer of 1816. One can surmise that the intimacy that grew between the two poets on that voyage around the lake also threw into relief the philosophical, and temperamental, differences between them, which would become more apparent at the end of the summer. Despite their friendship, they were very different. Even their physical deportment was different: Byron rather stiff and immobile (he hated to walk limping across a drawing room); Shelley all sinuous, restless movement (Byron called him "the snake" on account of this). If Byron could be aloof, his face a mask assumed to hide his true feelings, Shelley, with his headlong enthusiasm and erratic ardor, his large bright eyes agleam, was all outward expression. Shelley wrote then that Byron was "an exceedingly interesting person, and as such it is to be regretted that he is a slave to the vilest and most vulgar prejudices, and as mad as the winds." The prejudices may have referred to Byron's retrograde literary tastes (he thought Pope among the greatest English poets), the madness to Byron's aristocratical airs. There was also a hint of jealousy. Shelley felt that, great as Byron's achievements were— and he was more successful by far, in a commercial sense, than Shelley—Byron had not achieved what he was capable of. What most drew them together, apart from the feeling of kinship that must have arisen from the fact that each was regarded as an outcast in England, was a shared taste for irreverent humor. In 1822 Byron remembered "how we used to laugh now and then, at various things, which are grave in the suburbs."

By the time they met in Venice in 1818 there had been a marked divergence in their way of thinking. In the Third Canto of *Childe Harold*, written in that Swiss summer of 1816, Byron showed the influence of Shelley's thought, particularly in his avowals of faith in the transcendental operations of nature. He later complained that he had been dosed with Wordsworth "even to nausea." It was Shelley who administered the dose. In the Third Canto Byron had written of his hopes that his soul might "flee" from the world and its torments to "remount at last," free from "what it hates in this degraded form," to join with immortal nature. Are not, he asks, "the mountains, waves and skies, a part / Of me and of my soul, as I of them?" There is a sense in all this of Byron trying, not quite convinced, to force himself into a mood of transcendence, and a faith in nature's redemptive power, which he took from Shelley but which he did not truly feel. The language is stressed to support an emotion beyond its capacity. He wrote to Tom Moore in 1817 that he was "half mad during the time of its [ie, the Third Canto's] composition, between metaphysics, mountains, lakes, love inextinguishable, thoughts unutterable, and the nightmare of my own delinquencies."

Once he arrived in Italy and started work on the Fourth Canto, which was completed in 1817, Byron took a different stance from that assumed in the Third; in fact, a complete reversal. He now came to reject Shelley's vision of an imaginative faculty which enabled intuition of the unity of beauty and love. Byron now saw this as an illusion, the fruit of a diseased mind.. "Of its own beauty is the mind diseased / And fevers into false creation.." We are all helpless against the deep-rooted flaws in our nature. The "charms and virtues which we dare / Conceive in boyhood and pursue as men" are all the "unreach'd Paradise of our despair..." The emotions and the intellect, desire and consciousness, remain in perpetual conflict:

> Our life is a false nature: 'tis not in
> The harmony of things--this hard decree
> This uneradicable taint of sin,
> This boundless upas, this all-blasting tree
> Whose root is earth, whose leaves and branches be
> The skies which rain their plagues on men like dew.

Even love is an illusion ("who loves raves") and its ecstasy is doomed to end in bitterness and despair. The cure for love ("youth's frenzy")

> Is bitterer still: as charm by charm unwinds
> Which robed our idols, and we see too sure
> Nor worth nor beauty dwells from out the mind's
> Ideal shape of such yet still it binds
> The fatal spell, and still it draws us on...

There is no surcease from the woes, seen and unseen, which afflict the "immedicable soul." The only defense is hard thought, not the poetic imagination. Let us, he argues, "ponder boldly." It is a "base / Abandonment of reason to resign / Our right of thought--our last and only place / Of refuge..."

If we are fated to endure that upas tree, poisoning the air and ground around it, the only other recourse, apart from practical rationality, is defiance. Here Byron allows himself to show the hurt and resentment he still felt from ostracism and calumny and from being stared at and cut by English tourists for whom he was a scandalous celebrity:

> From mighty wrongs to petty perfidy
> Have I not seen what human things could do?
> From the loud roar of foaming calumny
> To the small whisper of the as paltry few,
> And subtler venom of the reptile crew...

On all of them he piles "the mountain of my curse."

Shelley saw all this as self-pity and needless despair. He wrote to Peacock about the Fourth Canto: "The spirit in which it is written is, if insane, the most wicked and mischievous insanity that ever was given forth. It is a kind of obstinate and self-willed folly in which he hardens himself."

When Shelley wrote this he was prepared to place the blame for these "expressions of contempt and desperation" on Byron's dissipated life in Venice. It does seem that as Byron travelled south he left behind in the Swiss mountains not only the pantheistic raptures of the Third Canto but also much of the gloom and guilt which followed his departure from England. In Venice he found the setting, as so many have before and since, for a more carefree, sensual and liberated mood.

To be sure, the Venice Byron found when he arrived in the winter of 1816 was not quite the place of gaiety and feverish dissipation that William Beckford had enjoyed in the 1780's. Since 1797, when the last Doge resigned and the Republic came to an end, Venice had declined to an obscure province of the Austrian empire. The air of seediness was to Byron's taste. "It has not disappointed me," he wrote to Tom Moore, "though its evident decay would, perhaps, have that effect upon others. But I have been familiar with ruins too long to dislike desolation."

The impression of imminent loss, of irrecoverable beauty in the course of vanishing, remains a part of the emotional response of every visitor to the city. In its watery element, seemingly hovering between sea and sky, the city has an air of evanescence, even of illusion. Thousands upon thousands of paintings have made the buildings and canals of Venice familiar to everyone, but without diminishing the aesthetic impact. Perhaps this is because what is affecting is not simply the visual discovery of a Venice anticipated by familiar paintings—works by artists as various as Canaletto and Turner— as the impression of constant fluid movement, like a mysteriously summoned musical theme. The city, particularly on the great canal or when seen from the lagoon, echoes with its rhythms and harmonies the sound of some dimly heard or half forgotten melody to which the slap of water and the cries of gondoliers add their notes.

Whatever Byron may have been thinking as his gondola approached the *bacino*, he soon found in Venice an emancipation from the resentful obsessions that had bedevilled his time in the Alps. He discovered, with a renewed zest for life in general, a revival of sensual appetite. "I know not how it is," he wrote to Moore, "my health growing better, and my spirits not worse, the *besoin d'aimer* came back upon my heart...and, after all, there is nothing like it."

Apart from more casual encounters Byron took as his mistresses, successively, two married women. The first (who became his mistress while he was living under the roof of her husband, before he moved to the Palazzo Mocenigo) was the tempestuous Marianna Segati. The second was Margarita Cogni, almost equally volatile. She was the wife of a baker ("La Fornarina"). Each of these women from the artisan class was strong, fiery, beautiful and illiterate--all of which appealed to Byron. But, with their incessant fights and tantrums, added to his other assignations and nights at balls and the Ridotto, his life must have been exhausting. Years later, in a conversation with Medwin, Byron regretted "plunging into a vortex that was anything but pleasure" in this period; but that comment was made after he had settled with Teresa Guiccioli. At about the time of Shelley's visit some were impressed by a deterioration in Byron's appearance and put it down to the life he led. He had run to fat again, was pale and flabby and his hair was thinner. With his graying curls, his outmoded clothes and the rings on his (now too plump) hands he must have resembled not so much Childe Harold as an ageing dandy. Even so, he was still athletic enough to win a swimming race across the lagoon.

There is something weirdly censorious, though, in Shelley's outrage, however *louche* Byron's style of life had become. Shelley finds Italian women "the most contemptible of all who exist under the moon." Apart from their lack of hygiene they (even Countesses!) "smell so of garlick that an ordinary Englishman cannot approach them." Shelley's revulsion at prostitution fuels his disgust. Byron is "familiar with the lowest sort of these women, the people his gondolier picks up in the streets. He allows fathers and mothers to bargain with him for their daughters, and though this is common enough in Italy, yet for an Englishman to encourage such sickening vice is a melancholy thing." In a possible reference to homosexuality or transvestism, Shelley writes that Byron "associates with wretches who seem almost to have lost the gait and physiognomy of man, and who do not scruple to avow practices which are not only not named but I believe seldom even conceived in England." With all this, Shelley asks, is it a surprise that Byron, with this distorted mirror, sees the nature and destiny of man reflected as he does, showing such objects of contempt and despair?

The opposition of the ideas and temperaments of Byron and Shelley, along with the attraction that bound them in friendship despite this, is found in one of Shelley's finest poems, *Julian and Maddalo*. Julian is Shelley. Count Maddalo is Byron. The setting is Venice. Maddalo is a pessimist and cynic; Julian an optimist who believes in human perfectibility. Julian argues "against despondency, but pride / Made my companion take the darker side." If Maddalo, as described in Shelley's prose preface to the poem, has "an intense apprehension of the nothingness of life," he is nevertheless cheerful, frank and witty. "His more serious conversation is a sort of intoxication; men are held by it as by a spell." Julian, an atheist, is an ameliorist who "without concealing the evil in the world...is forever speculating how good may be made superior."

The two go riding on the Lido, as Byron and Shelley did. In a letter to Mary in Bagni di Lucca Shelley describes going in Byron's gondola across the lagoon to the "long sandy island which defends Venise [sic] from the Adriatic." There they found the horses waiting for them and rode along the sands, talking. "Our conversation consisted," Shelley writes, "in histories of his wounded feelings, and questions as to my affairs, and great professions of friendship and regard for me...We talked of literary matters..."

The Lido was then, as Shelley describes it in the poem, "a bare strand / Of hillocks, heaped from ever-drifting sand, / Matted with thistles and amphibious weeds." This was long before the luxury hotels were built there with their bathing cabins and deck chairs (where, a century later but a world away, Thomas Mann's weary Aschenbach would gaze longingly at the youthful Tadzio). "I love," as Shelley has Julian say, "all waste / And solitary places; where we taste / The pleasure of believing what we see / Is boundless, as we wish our souls to be..." As they ride the two poets recapture the atmosphere of that summer on the lake two years before when they had talked late into the night:

> So as we rode, we talked; and the swift thought,
> Winging itself with laughter, lingered not
> But flew from brain to brain,--such glee was ours,
> Charged with light memories of remembered hours,
> None slow enough for sadness...

(No mention of Byron's wounded feelings, then.)

Returning across the lagoon the pair pass by an island on which there is a lunatic asylum. Julian scoffs at the bell calling the inmates to prayer. In an exchange (which, if it occurred in fact, must have reminded them both of the boating accident off the rocks at Meillerie) Maddalo rebukes Julian's infidelity: "if you can't swim / Beware of Providence." Julian looks at Maddalo, "But the gay smile had faded in his eye."

Calling on Maddalo's palace the next day Julian finds Maddalo's daughter. Julian had "nursed / Her fine and feeble limbs when she came first / To this bleak world.." which was almost true of Shelley and Allegra. In continuing his argument with Maddalo Julian uses the child ("innocent...free...with little care") as an example of the state from which we came and to which we must aspire (more "dosing" with Wordsworth?). "You talk Utopia," Maddalo replies brusquely. To hammer home his point Maddalo cites the case of a Maniac, "one like you...With whom I argued in this sort, and he / Is now gone mad..." He takes Julian to the asylum where the

Maniac is confined. There, amid "Moans, shrieks and curses and blaspheming prayers" they meet the Maniac.

In his prose preface Shelley described the Maniac as a man disappointed in love, whose story "told at length, might be like many other stories of the same kind." But the prolonged recitation by the Maniac is almost incoherent in contrast with the cool impartiality of the rest of the poem. It is a tale of rejection (the Maniac seems to clutch at a letter from his former beloved) but also stained with images of sexual torment, even self-castration. After this exhausting performance the Maniac falls asleep. Maddalo and Julian return to Maddalo's Palace where they talk until dawn. Julian focuses on lost love at the root of the Maniac's suffering. For Maddalo such suffering is part of the human lot. "Most wretched men / Are cradled into poetry by wrong / They learn in suffering what they teach in song."

There is no doubt that the themes of sexual frustration, confinement and madness were much on the minds of both poets at the time. As in the past with their reflections on Prometheus and Rousseau, they found themselves working on parallel lines. In April 1817 Byron had visited the cell in Ferrara where Torquato Tasso had been confined for seven years by Alphonso d' Este and Byron's *Lament of Tasso* was the result. In the poem Tasso reflects on his love for the Princess Leonora, his suffering and threatened madness among other madmen in the Hospital of Sant Anna ("Above me, hark! the long and maniac cry / Of minds and bodies in captivity"). The poem is about the effect of long imprisonment on the human spirit, especially where the punishment is meted out to one whose only fault is love--the "very love which lock'd me to my chain / Hath lightn'd half its weight." Tasso implores Leonora to tell the Prince, her brother, that Tasso's heart remains "untamed" and he adores her still. He consoles himself with the thought that his fame will outlast that of the Prince.

At about the same time Shelley was embarked on the composition of a verse drama about Tasso which also engaged the themes of isolation, imprisonment, madness and frustrated love. Tasso is shown in his prison conjuring up the spirit of Leonora "Till by the grated casement's ledge / It fades..." This was on Shelley's mind when he visited Byron in Venice; in fact, his play included a poet called Count Maddalo.

Is the Maniac, then, just another Tasso? While the plight of Tasso, as depicted in both Byron's poem and Shelley's unfinished play, is clearly the inspiration for the Maniac, Shelley seems to have incorporated in the Maniac's ravings elements of the complaints of both poets. There seems to me to be a deliberate paradox here.

At the Palazzo, before the trip to the madhouse, Julian argued that if man were the "passive thing" Maddalo believed then religion would be adequate to "break a teachless nature to the yoke." But, he argues with the example of the happy child before him, "it is our will / That thus enchains us to permitted ill--/ We might be otherwise...Where is the love, beauty and truth we seek / But in our mind?" We might find that the chains which bind our spirit, once tried, are as brittle as straw. We have power over ourselves to achieve "something nobler than to live or die." Maddalo offers the Maniac as an example ("one like you...With whom I argued in this sort...") and a refutation. But the Maniac, once we are introduced to his cell, raves in the voice of the Byron of the Fourth Canto of *Childe Harold* ("The thorns which I have reaped are of the tree / I planted: they have torn me and I bleed"). The Maniac is both a reflection and a criticism of Byron himself. (The Maniac seems to rebuke Byron indirectly as one of the "perverted beings" who "think to find / In scorn or hate a medicine for the mind / Which scorn or hate have wounded...") While Maddalo wants to prove that indulgence in Shelleyan Utopianism leads to madness, Shelley has manipulated the situation to show us in the Maniac a tormented, despairing Byronic hero. And yet, as suggested by Shelley's biographer Richard Holmes, some of the Maniac's ravings appear to suggest that he is an expression of Shelley's own unhappiness and guilt; and may refer to Mary's bitterness after the death of their son William that summer, Shelley's affair with Claire, even guilt at the death of Harriet. That may be so, but when Shelley adapted Byron's thorny metaphor in his *Ode to the West Wind*, written two years after the encounter in Venice, it was not his own actions but the weight of mortality itself which oppressed him: "I fall upon the thorns of life! I bleed!"

Was Shelley, in the Maniac's monologue, adopting the rhetorical devices of Byron to say to his friend, in effect, "I too have suffered terribly but unlike the poor Maniac, and unlike you, will survive with my ideals intact"? This may be suggested as the poem concludes with the image of a growing child, symbol of hope renewed. Years after the earlier visit Julian returns to Venice. Maddalo has left for Armenia and "his dog was dead." (Byron was taking lessons in the Armenian language in Venice.) The Maniac's lover had returned to visit him and he had died. The little girl appears again. She has become a fine woman. The poem ends abruptly.

*   *   *

Allegra, alas! would never grow to womanhood. She died of fever at the age of five in a convent near Ravenna. If Byron did not mourn her for long, he cannot be blamed for her death. The Shelleys lost two children, William, the beloved "Wilmouse," and the baby Clara from the same cause in Italy, and Mary was not a neglectful mother.

Shelley's poem stands as an epitaph to the association between the two poets which sprang up in the summer of 1816. Henceforth, their connection, however personally close, would be different. While remaining friends, each recognized the growing distance. Byron was already working in a new idiom. He wrote to Murray, referring to *Beppo*, that he could now show his readers "that I can write cheerfully and repel the charge of monotony and mannerism." At the time of his meeting with Shelley in Venice Byron had already started work on what was to be his greatest production, the satirical epic *Don Juan*, completing the move from bitterness and anger through Stoicism to a redemptive humor and hatred of cant.

With *Don Juan* Childe Harold has, finally, entered a thoroughly adult world, a mature world in which wit, gaiety and despair were blended. Not only the tone but the manner is unlike anything Byron had previously written. The language is colloquial—it is the language of Byron's letters and journals—reflecting the speech of a witty man of the world. One can easily imagine Byron sitting up late at night, fortified by gin-and-water, effectively talking in verse as he wrote. The *ottava rima* form which Byron chose permitted a loose, fast-paced, irregular and expansive narrative flow; with a final couplet well adapted to epigram, which Byron employed to great effect

To complete the transformation from his early Venetian way of life, by April, 1819, Byron had met the Countess Guiccioli and soon settled down as her permanent lover and *cicisbeo*. His days of random whoring were over. "I am in love," he wrote, "and tired of promiscuous concubinage." As for the relationship with Shelley, Byron was to write in 1822 that "poor Shelley" was the "least selfish and the mildest of men" though "with his speculative opinions I have nothing in common, nor desire to have." Byron always ranked Shelley high as a poet "but for his unfortunate predilection for metaphysics..." Shelley found, by 1821, that Byron had "greatly improved...in moral views," due to the influence of Teresa Guiccioli and had "got rid of all those melancholy and degrading habits which he indulged at Venice." But whatever influence Shelley may have had over Byron's thought and work did not outlast the summer of 1816.

*   *   *

Years before Shelley had written: "I think one is always in love with something or other; the error, and I confess it is not easy for spirits cased in flesh and blood to avoid it, consists in seeking in a mortal image the likeness of what is perhaps eternal." Shelley believed in love as a philosophical concept, sharing Plato's view of love as a divine universal lying outside time and change. Our experience of it ascends from love for an individual to the contemplation of love itself, from a live passion to an abstraction. This was Shelley's secular version of the idea embraced by Renaissance neo-Platonists like Pietro Bembo--that carnal love leads step by step to ideal love in which passion is harnessed by the intellect, ascending to perfect love which, in their case, meant love of God. But, as Shelley found, this Platonic love is difficult in practice. If the sentiment provides its own justification, the ascent to ideal love may be careless of the happiness or welfare of the person who originally inspired it. The more Shelley embraced his ideal of love the more likely it was to result in his lovers' dissatisfaction.

Byron made fun of this Platonic view of love when he wrote in *Don Juan* of Plato as a kind of pimp ("no better than a go-between"):

> Oh Plato! Plato! you have paved the way,
> With your confounded fantasies, to more
> Immoral conduct by the fancied sway
> Your system feigns o'er the controlless core
> Of human hearts, than all the long array
> Of poets and romancers...

Shelley's Platonic notion of love seemed to degenerate, in his personal life, into a vagueness, especially when he fell into a rather ridiculous passion for Emilia Viviani. He seemed at that time to see love almost like a beneficial gas in the atmosphere; there could not be too much of it. Unlike misery, which was reduced by being divided, love expanded with division.

> I never was attached to that great sect,
> Whose doctrine is, that each one should select
> Out of the crowd a mistress or a friend,
> And all the rest, though fair and wise, commend
> To cold oblivion...

and

Love is like understanding, that grows bright
Gazing on many truths...

(*Epipsychidion*)

That attitude had made Mary quite miserable at times when Shelley seemed to be going away from her, and it may be that for Shelley love really was a means of escape from worrisome everyday realities. There was unhappiness along with illness (Mary had miscarried and almost died) as well as hallucinations and premonitory nightmares in that house at Lerici with the waves crashing on the shore.

Shelley's poetic genius was always at its highest when least didactic and declamatory and least involved in rhetorical abstractions, though the language is sometimes strangely moving even when the meaning is obscure. At its best his words show an extraordinary depth of feeling beautifully expressed. I remember once, I must have been about fifteen, reading a passage which made me shudder--the power of the words had an impact which was physical. I cannot recall what the words were, and they would almost certainly not have the same effect now, but I can think of few other poets whose words have brought about this response. Though there was no weakening of his poetic abilities Shelley may, near the end of his life, have begun to question his faith in the inevitable triumph of his ideals. If man's wickedness was a result of his own willfulness, could man escape his fallen nature? If Shelley had begun to question his former beliefs, he seems to have felt the need to return to Rousseau for new inspiration.

*   *   *

What now of that Rousseau, whose Julie had so entranced both Byron and Shelley as they climbed the hill at Clarens in 1816? Byron, we may suppose, was less convinced by such exaggerated passion as that of Julie and St Preux. Disillusionment would follow. Byron's Julia may be seen as a riposte to this; yielding to her obsessive desire for the young Don Juan she ends up shut in a nunnery by her jealous husband while Juan escapes to further adventures. If love is the world for a woman a man's fulfillment is found in engagement and action. In a humorous note of October 1821 he derided any similarity (as Mme de Stael, and others, had maintained) between himself and Rousseau: "He wrote prose, I verse; he was of the people, I of the Aristocracy; he was a philosopher, I am none...he married his housekeeper, I could not keep house with my wife...he could never ride nor swim...I am an excellent swimmer, a decent though not at all a dashing rider..not a bad boxer when I could keep my temper... Besides, Rousseau's way of life, his country, his manners, his whole character, were so very different, that I am at a loss to conceive how such a comparison could have arisen...I forgot to say that he was also short-sighted and that hitherto my eyes have been the contrary," and so on. While this catalogue of superficial differences is frivolous, Byron makes it plain that he is not pleased with the "chimera" that he resembles Rousseau in thought or sentiment and, indeed, it is hard to imagine anything further from Byron's attitude to life than the pathetic simplicity of Rousseau.

By 1822 Shelley too had lost some of his infatuation with the Rousseau he embraced with such abandonment in 1816. Rousseau was now, for Shelley, implicated in Enlightenment rationalism, the "cold light" which distorted what it fell upon. But it was not as a philosopher but as a visionary poet and guide that Rousseau first attracted Shelley and as such Shelley returns to him in *The Triumph of Life*, that strange poem which Shelley left unfinished when he died in July.

In the poem Shelley, the narrator, after a sleepless night, falls into a trance and has a dream or vision. He sees a confused multitude, a great stream of people of all ages hurrying onward, though none seems to know "whither he went or whence he came." They flee before a chariot which arrives bearing a "shape" which turns out to be Rousseau. Rousseau's form is now distorted like an old root.

He is an ancient ghost who now plays Virgil to Shelley's Dante. He offers to "unfold that which to this deep scorn led him and his companions in the pageant". Rousseau identifies the shades of the great and wise assembled, as in a Roman triumph, before the chariot of time--Roman Emperors, Popes, Voltaire, Catherine the Great. Frederick the Great, Napoleon, even Plato and Aristotle. Shelley, "sick of this perpetual flow" demands that Rousseau explain his posthumous history. Rousseau describes an hallucinatory encounter with a mysterious woman. He demands that she tell him "whence I came and where I am and why." She bids him drink from her cup. "Suddenly," he says, "my brain became as sand...upon the shore." There is revealed to him not just the men and women falling beneath the chariot but phantoms, ambitions, ideas and visions too--"Mask after mask fell from the countenance / And form of all." Nothing, even the constructs of the mind, escapes oblivion. Then what is life? Shelley demands.

The MS breaks off here, before Rousseau can answer. The back of the sheet is covered with sketches of sails--to be added to Shelley's already over-rigged boat, the *Ariel*, which went down with him a few weeks later. Shelley had reached a point of crisis at this time. He may have been on the verge of a new intellectual departure--or suffering a collapse of faith, or both. In one of his last letters from Lerici he wrote: "I stand, as it were, upon a precipice, which I have ascended with great, and I cannot descend without greater, peril."

It is touching that at this point he summoned the ghost of that Rousseau he had encountered in the rainy summer of 1816. But this Rousseau appears to be a messenger of disappointment, witness to the evanescent nature of Shelley's early ideals, what Byron now dismissed as his "metaphysics." Is Shelley admitting that these notions, derived from Wordsworth, Plato, Rousseau himself--that in the contemplation of nature the mind of man and the universe become a great whole; that all that partakes of beauty approaches to a universal spirit of love-- like mask after mask, these ideas and visions too must fall? Alas, Shelley did not live to give Rousseau voice to answer.

XV

Epilogue

If that summer in 1816 affected all those who gathered at Montalegre or in the Villa Diodati or went on boating parties on the lake, it was on Mary's memory they were most deeply imprinted. It seems to have been the powerful personality of Byron that came to the forefront of her mind when she cast her memory back on those times. On the anniversary of the meeting of Shelley and Byron at Secheron she wrote in her journal: "I am melancholy after reading the Third Canto of *Childe Harold*. Do you remember, Shelley, when you first read it to me? One evening after returning from Diodati. It was in our little room at Chapuis--the lake was before us...Dear Lake! I shall ever love thee. How a powerful mind can sanctify past scenes and recollections...To think of our excursions on the lake--how we saw him when he came down to us, or welcomed our arrival with a good-humoured smile. How very vividly does each verse of his poem recall some scene of this kind to my memory." Mary indulged her nostalgia for the joys and excitements of that summer by reading Rousseau's *Julie* exactly one year after Byron and Shelley went on their boat tour of the lake with the novel as their companion.

Mary's memories of that time recurred again and again as death removed the company one by one. Dr Polidori killed himself with a massive dose of Prussic Acid in 1821. Shelley was drowned in July 1822. In October of that year Mary recalled in her journal the voices of Byron (Albe) and Shelley in their late night conversations beside the lake:

I do not think that any person's voice has the same power of awakening melancholy in me as Albe's--I have been accustomed when hearing it to listen and to speak little--another voice, not mine, ever replied, a voice whose strings are broken; and when Albe ceases to speak I expect to hear that other voice, and when I hear another instead it jars strangely with every association. I have seen so little of Albe since our residence in Switzerland, and having seen him there every day his voice, a peculiar one, is engraved on my memory with other sounds and objects from which it can never disunite itself...since incapacity and timidity always prevented my mingling in the nightly conversation at Diodati [surely, Mary is being too modestly self-effacing here?]--they were, as it were, entirely tete a tete between my Shelley and Albe and thus, as I have said--when Albe speaks and Shelley does not answer, it is as thunder without rain, the form of the sun without heat or light, as any familiar object might be shorn of its dearest and best attribute--and I listen with an unspeakable melancholy--that yet is not all pain.

The pain, though, was there, and in another entry Mary invokes, in a haunting reference, her horror at the watery element that sucked the life from her husband: "When in company with Albe I can never cease for a second to have him [Shelley] in my heart and brain with a clearness that mocks reality, interfering ever by its force with the functions of life--until if tears do not relieve me the hysterical feeling, analogous to that which the murmur of sea gives me, presses painfully upon me."

Byron died at Missolonghi in April 1824 and hearing of his death sent Mary back to her journal. On May 15th she wrote:

Byron has become one of the people of the grave--that immeasurable conclave to which the beings I best love

belong. I knew him in the bright days of youth, when
neither care nor fear had visited me: before death had
made me feel my mortality and the earth was the scene
of my hopes--Can I forget our evening visits to Diodati-
-our excursions on the lake when he sang the Tyrolean
hymn--and his voice was harmonized with winds and
waves? Can I forget his attentions and consolations to me
during my deepest misery?--Never.

In 1840, eleven years before her own death, Mary paid a final visit
to the lake. She was then the sole survivor, except for Claire, who
lived on until 1879. (At the time of her death Claire was a semi-
recluse in Florence; it was a story about her and her supposed hoard
of literary treasure, and a treasure-seeker, which inspired Henry
James' *The Aspern Papers*.) Mary left the companions with whom
she was traveling. ("I had a whim," she wrote, "to go to Vevay [sic],
and make the voyage in the steamer.") It was October, and cold.
"The far Alps were hid; the wide lake looked drear." In spite of this,
Mary managed to see what she had come for:

At length, I caught a glimpse of the scenes among which
I had lived, when first I stepped out from childhood into
life. There, on the shores of Bellerive, stood Diodati; and
our humble dwelling Maison Chapuis, nestled close to
the lake below. There were the terraces, the vineyards,
the upward path threading them, the little port where our
boat lay moored; I could mark and recognise a thousand
slight peculiarities, familiar objects then--forgotten since-
-now replete with recollections and associations. Was I
the same person who had lived there, the companion of
the dead? For all were gone: even my young child, whom
I had looked upon as the joy of future years, had died in
infancy--not one hope, then in fair bud, had opened into
maturity; storm, and blight, and death, had passed over,
and destroyed all. While yet very young, I had reached
the position of an aged person driven back on memory

for companionship with the beloved; and now I looked
on the inanimate objects that had surrounded me, which
survived the same in aspect as then, to feel that all my
life since was but an unreal phantasmagoria--the shades
that gathered round that scene were the realities--the
substance and truth of the soul's life, which I shall, I
trust, hereafter rejoin.

Disappointed in her voyage, "for it was dreary," Mary proceeded on
to Geneva and took refuge in the Hotel des Bergues.

*   *   *

Back in Geneva I spent my last evening walking along the quai.
The summer was over. I arrived in Geneva a week ago and, after a
week of rain it is autumn. There is a chill in the air and dead leaves
cluttered the paths at Voltaire's chateau at Ferney. Here in Geneva,
on the Pont du Mt Blanc, I feel the Rhone throbbing under my
feet. Behind the hills beyond Cologny the full moon rises, a golden
globe. I can almost feel the world turning, minute by minute. The
signs over the grand hotels shine along the quai, and I treat myself
to the last ice cream cone of the year.

As my voyage round the lake neared its end I was struck by how
my tour, in some respects and unintentionally, seemed to have
taken the form of an exploration of different attitudes to love.
From Rousseau, with his balance of passion and conscience
at one end of the lake, the doctrine of feeling migrated to the
torments and histrionics of Mme de Stael and Benjamin Constant
at the other, by way of Shelley's philosophy and practice of love;
and Byron's clear-eyed detachment, recognizing the depth of
passion but always looking for the insincerity hidden at the
root of it.

Of course these reflections had nothing to do with my childhood
memories which were occasioned in the course of the trip. My

encounters with love in the adult sense--in all its usual varieties of exalted passion, erotic power, deep attachment or even mental derangement--came to me later. But, still, there is a kind of love we learn as children and which I was aware of as I cruised the lake. In that case the lesson is that love is not an end but a process by which one person knows another. It is neither a state of grace nor an illusion but an act of becoming, a condition modified day by day by the intelligence and the heart. The person one loves at first is not the person one loves at last. Nor is the lover the same. This is a love which matures and changes as we grow up.

The week passed on the lake was sombre, and not just because of the weather. It was a week passed mainly in the company of ghosts--Rousseau, Byron and Shelley, Mme de Stael and Benjamin Constant. Not only these historic shades but the ghosts of those who had been closest to me in my early life. In the course of my journey around the lake, with my two romantic poets, memories of my childhood self have intruded like an insistent fellow-passenger interrupting the story. I have been sadly conscious at times, particularly at Vevey, of being the only survivor of my childhood family. There is no one to whom I can say, do you remember that... thing or person or event? The urge to share a memory sometimes, as here, exerts a pressure within me, a pressure which cannot be relieved by any effort of recollection.

One cannot go back, of course, but I have also learned that the memories which are most real--that actually do recapture the past in the Proustian sense--are tangential to normal daily experience. They come unbidden. One cannot force memory. It is odd, though, the springs from which rivers of nostalgia flow. Once, in a museum looking at old Chinese paintings, I found a poem, a meditation by an elderly monk exiled to a mountain retreat, as painted on a piece of silk by an emperor of the thirteenth century, five centuries after the poem was composed. For some reason the memory of my parents, and the lake under the mountains, came to me forcibly. The translation was on the label:

163

Still I yearn to see my parents in every crowd
Here white clouds always touch the eastern mountains
Sitting alone I burn incense and recite sutras
The mountain is deep, the temple ancient, and snow
everywhere.

As for having no one with whom to share certain memories, that is simply why people become more inward as they grow older--until death which is, of course, the ultimate solitary experience.

I am glad to leave, glad to be able to leave, glad to feel that there is still so much before that I need not lose myself in what has gone. In a few hours I shall be back in London.

RH Lloyd
Geneva, London, Oklahoma—2009 – 2013

Bibliographical Note

I have quoted liberally from the works, published letters and journals of the literary figures referred to in this memoir. In addition, I have relied on the following biographies:

Cranston, Maurice: *Jean-Jacques, The Early Life and Work of Jean-Jacques Rousseau, 1712-1754* (1983).

Cranston, Maurice: *The Noble Savage, Jean-Jacques Rousseau, 1754-1762* (1991).

Damrosch, Leo: *Jean-Jacques Rousseau, Restless Genius* (2007).

Fairweather, Maria: *Madame de Stael* (2005).

Fothergill, Brian: *Beckford of Fonthill* (1979).

Gerin, Winifred: *Horatia Nelson* (1970).

Herold, J Christopher: *Mistress to an Age; A Life of Madame de Stael* (1958).

Holmes, Richard: *Shelley; The Pursuit* (1974).

MacCarthy, Fiona: *Byron, Life and Legend* (2002).

Nicolson, Harold: *Benjamin Constant* (1949).

Origo, Iris: *The Last Attachment* (1949)

Quennell, Peter, *Byron in Italy* (1941).

Scott, Geoffrey: *The Portrait of Zelide* (1927).

Seymour, Miranda: *Mary Shelley* (2001).

Illustrations

The author and his sister before and after the War--at Mansfield Road, Oxford in 1940 and at Sunningwood, Boars Hill, in 1946.

The author's parents, Martha and Edward, Oxford 1940.

The Grand Hotel de Vevey, as it was. Musee Historique de Vevey, 1800 Vevey, Suisse.

The portrait of Lord Byron by Richard Westall (1813) is reproduced by permission of The National Portrait Gallery, London. It shows Byron at the height of his London fame and—loose collar, distant gaze, pallor and all—at his most characteristic.

The Villa Diodati, Cologny, Geneva, in 2009; author photo.

Lord Byron at the Villa Deodati in 1816. A print (c 1820) in the collection of the New York Public Library.

The Chateau de Chillon in a turbulent Lake with the Dents du Midi in the distance. From a post card. By permission of Photo Perrochet SA, Lausanne.

This Illustration ("Le Premier Baiser de l'Amour") by Hubert Francois
Gravelot is from the 1760 edition of J-J Rousseau's *Julie ou La Nouvelle
Heloise* in the Beinecke Library, Yale University.

The view of Edward Gibbon's Pavilion and Terrace at Lausanne engraved by Charles Heath (1785-1848) for an edition of Gibbon's Miscellaneous Works, vol III (1815).

Percy Bysshe Shelley

This sketch of Shelley (in the Pierpont Morgan Library) was made by Edward Williams some time not long before their fatal voyage in Shelley's boat, the *Ariel*, in the summer of 1822.

Apart from his portrait as a boy (c. 1802) Shelley only sat for one formal portrait, that done by Amelia Curran in Rome in May 1819. That portrait, now in the National Portrait Gallery, London, remained in Rome until it was delivered to Mary Shelley in 1825. Mary thought it was "unfinished" and not a good likeness, though it was used as the basis for later (probably idealized) images of Shelley in his posthumously published works.

Certainly Williams' sketch, if every bit as amateurish as the Curran portrait, better conveys the intensity one thinks of as being characteristic of Shelley.

"Ah, did you once see Shelley plain…" [Browning]

[The Pierpont Morgan Library, New York, Gift of Mrs W Murray Crane, 1949. 1949.3. Photography by Steven Crossot, 2014]

View of the Chateau de la Tour de Peilz from Vevey. Watercolor painting by MV Brandoin (1758-1844). Musee Historique de Vevey, 1800 Vevey, Suisse.

View of the Chateau de Coppet at the time of Madame de Stael. Collection of the Chateau de Coppet, Vaud.

This portrait of a Sybil by Domenichino was painted c 1620-25. Domenichino painted at least two other Sybils—one of them in the Borghese Gallery in Rome. They depict the same exotic costumes and elaborate head dresses. This painting belonged to the Regent of France, Philippe duc d'Orleans and later to his descendant, Philippe Egalite. It was purchased by the Marquess of Hertford and is now in The Wallace Collection, London, and is reproduced here by kind permission of the Trustees of the Wallace Collection.

The portrait of Mme de Stael by Francois Gerard is at the Chateau de Coppet. It was commissioned by her children and painted after her death in 1817. She holds a green twig--it was her custom to toy with a twig as she spoke. Collection of the Chateau de Coppet.

The painting by George Romney of Emma Hart, Lady Hamilton, as Calypso (1791-2) is at Waddesdon Manor, The Rothschild Collection (The National Trust), bequest of James de Rothschild, 1957, acc no 2469, and is reproduced with their consent. © The National Trust, Waddesden Manor.

This portrait of Mary Shelley by Richard Rothwell was shown at the Royal Academy in 1840, the year in which Mary made her last visit to the Lake. National Portrait Gallery, London.